DREAM
of
BROKEN
FEATHERS

JEFF EDRICH

Also by Jeff Edrich

When the Sun Touched the River
Iron in the Country

Available from Amazon.com books
Visit website: www.jeffedrich.com
Email: jeff.edrich@yahoo.com

Cover Design by Kit Foster
www.kitfosterdesign.com
ISBN-13: 978-0-9883589-0-4

In memory of a soul
who came to heal the world
and after embracing us all
left to become the stars and the wind

CONTENTS

II

Before You Are Gone

When you can no longer see,
and your eyes are white glows of inner knowing,
I will sit with you.

When your hands can no longer find the wooden spoon,
or the giving bowl,
I will guide them.

When barely a word can be spoken,
and gentle breaths are the songs of your voice,
I will press my ear close to your mouth and listen,
and each breath will be like sweet honey,
because you are inside them.

Feathers of My Ancestors

There are feathers around my neck.
We dance in the circle.

Silent voices rise, like mist from the dark lake,
pulling out the roots from hidden stores of memory,
their old emotion full, birthing fires into the sleeping dream.

They are all there, swimming in currents of blood,
freezing the world while their moment replays,
their thick presence holding its grasp.

The sharp touch of their knowing,
stripping the last cloth from skin.

I cannot hide, as those who have walked through my life,
reach out their arms and bind us together for eternity.

The feathers glow with translucent brightness.
The hypnotic movement of our tribal dance parts the veil.

In the space between the two worlds,
compassion crosses the river,
and life pours like water from her skin.

Under the cover of her warm wings,
I surrender, and the souls of my life return...

I am the one, who ran to you as a child,
knocking you to the ground laughing.
I am the one who lost my life by your hand.

I am the one who held my arms open, while you turned away.
I am the one you carried, when I could no longer walk.
I am the one who destroyed your life.
I am the one who never left your side.

Standing like the stars were my hands,
I look up to see what is the sky.
The sky is not above me,
and I cannot remember my name.

There are feathers around my neck.
We dance in the circle.

They speak, like smoke and thunder,
pressing through the concealed worlds,
into the night fire.

The voices move and scatter,
like leaves with a will of their own,
threading through our dance,
pulling up to the center of the knowing sky.

And one last voice...
clear...like the open water lake of falling snow... speaks...

I am the one,
who loved you long ago,
and brought you to a lake,
and washed your skin...

...so you could see your reflection,
and know how beautiful you were,
and how much I loved you,

and how beautiful it was,
when the sun touched the river,
and we became two fires on the water.

I am the one,
who was with you before you came,
and will be with you forever.

Always

In between the sun and moon,
two birds are on the water.

One is gone.

The teapot is whistling,
the chair is empty.

Wherever I am,
I hear the song of your life.

The Dreams in My Store

I have the rest of you on a shelf.
I don't know whether you were born without it,
or lost it along the way,
but whatever happened,
I have the rest of you here.

Come and get it.

It has been here since you were born,
holding promise.

I am not sure why you did not take it with you.
But not to worry,
it will be here tomorrow,
and every day, until you die.

Then we will clear the shelf and make room,
for the others who have left so much of themselves behind.

And make sure you pick this one,
the one with your name on it.

Where did you go?
Oh, I thought you were leaving,
I know, it is strange to look at the rest of you.

I know one other thing too… sometimes it is hard,
and you have to run away.

That's what usually happens.
I call out after them,
but they are a little frightened and can't hear,
so I keep the rest of them in case they want to come back
and get it. I keep the rest of them safe until the last day.

Usually I know they are gone,
because the rest of them just disappears from the shelf.
I don't see it very often, but sometimes it happens.

I'll just be cleaning up the shop, and while I happen to be
cleaning the shelf, the rest of them will disappear,
right in front of my eyes.

I don't know why, but I cry when that happens.
You would think I would be more jaded after all these years.
But I am not.

It is somehow sad, but also beautiful at the same time,
knowing they have been released from life,
like trees releasing their beautiful leaves,
and flowers releasing their floating seeds into the wind.

I am rambling now, I guess that's why I should keep busy.
My friend, we don't know each other, but somehow,
I am weeping for you.

When I see your artistry lying on the shelf here,
I dream of what you might have brought into the world,
and when I step over to this shelf and see
the ability to understand the ways of stars and light,
I wonder what you would have unfolded.

I am so foolish, all these parts of you lying on my shelves,
they are gifts. Why did I not simply say that from the start?
Because I am old and talk too much.

All right, one more thing before I say goodbye,
for I too will someday go.

I just wanted to let you know,
that I left without the rest of me too.

That happened a while back,
and one day when my heart was broken,
I cried so hard, I couldn't remember my name.

Then I saw my own gift that I had left on the shelf
and took it back, or embraced it for the first time, I should say.

Do you know what it was?
It was the glasses of the heart.
I couldn't feel anything before and ran roughshod over the world.
Now I feel everything and am touched by every breath and quiver.

I think I need to be somewhere in the middle, don't you?
It is a life of sorrow feeling the weight of all your tears.

Okay, I'll stop. I always get into trouble when I go on like that.
Oh, you are still here - I mean, the rest of you is still here.

Goddess

Once I lived in the forest.

The heat of your fire
entwined veins of light around my skin.
I had seen the star woman they would say.

Within dreams you appeared,
moving the world.
Painting the slain wolf at your feet,
watching the river melt into the delta.

The hay in your hands sparkled pure.
The hot embrace of your eyes,
opened into waves of warm wind.

Across the golden fields of harvest,
your sails filled in the setting sun.

Horse

He brushed the back of the horse in long strokes,
smoothing the hills and valleys,
as if she were trees and lakes and he the soft wind.

He brushed her shoulders, and cleaned the bottom of her hooves.
She stood close and pressed in towards him so they were touching.

To him, she was the leaves and the rivers and the sun,
all pressed tight together in the form of a horse.

She would run and stop to look at him,
pumping her head up and down,
and they would ride until they forgot they were not one.

As he brushed her, she snuffled into his underarm, nudging.
He laughed and embraced her big head until it was time
to close the stable door.

He wandered to the edge of the field.
The valley spread below like a wonder of sun and charm.

"May I go into the valley?" he wondered.
A voice said "No," and took the last leaf from his hand.

He yearned for the beckoning world,
but was caught in the current of endless days.

Why had these years run their course so quickly,
with so little fruit on the tree, like lives lost
in the wind of their time? His eyes closed.
He'd never have to face the sun again.

Something throbbed, like a bird trying to free itself and fly
through his skin. His blood suddenly arched up
and ran to push away from the sad weight of his bones.

A voice asked, "Why are you leaving?"

He wondered who had spoken, and opened his eyes slowly,
unsure, squinting, as if he had never seen before.

Everything was bright.
He shook his head to clear his vision and looked down.
The universe was in the grass,
his strong hands were shining in the sun.

No longer shrunken like a dead plant,
the wild river had found its home and flowed across
the amber lit fields and over the fences.

Into a dream suddenly real,
he felt himself waving with the grain and jumped from the cliff.

He threw his wings open,
born from the eternal hand of his hidden dream.

The horse came running alongside him
motioning with her bowing head.
He sailed upon her back,
and she could feel the rush of his light,

their two spirits together like a fire of wind-struck hammers
ringing out the clash of sun breaking through morning.

Down the high hill he rode,
slicing open the whispering secrets of the tall grass,
soft along the racing heat of her gallop,

Swinging one arm over his head,
calling the stars into his hand,
they fell into the world, like the waking rain of fire.

Innocent

When I dream of you, you are a little girl,
soft and shy, looking down at the ground,
embarrassed about something,
afraid to look up and see the sky,
or to show us your face.

As if you are afraid you might be scolded
for enjoying yourself.

You are beautiful, but no one tells you,
so you do not look up.

And sometimes, you are older,
a woman, having had children,
and I see you,
looking down, afraid to talk,

trying to hide while standing in a line,
or trying to disappear, so deeply within yourself,
that we would never be able to find you.

The Bridge Between Two Breaths

The water waits outside the window, whispering my name.
I surrender.

Through the walls and floor, a wave washes into the room
and pulls back into the sea.

I wake on the shore alone.
A star moves slowly across the daytime sky.

I am full with soft joy sitting alone in this day,
brushing the warm sand back and forth,
letting it run through my hand,
feeling the wonder of its tiny grains.

I am over the ocean, half in the day and half in the night.

Soft wind rustles the old leaves of memory.
I am inside them again.

My mother puts a glass of milk on the kitchen table.
I am bringing my wife a cup of tea.
Our children sit on the living room floor.

"What are stars?" they ask.

We open our hands and they swirl into the room,
and prayers and dreams fill the wind.

"Do you want some tea?" she asks.
I move toward her. We are tightly pressed together
gasping as if we had been running for miles.

Within the warmth of our blood, I dissolve,
following wings into the night high above the day.
I understand what I am seeing.

The constellation of the ancient drawbridge.
The door of the universe.
The beginning of everything that can be known.

The drawbridge begins to lower.
Something is about to exist with the same rights as light
and darkness.

I am watching the history of a soul.

The star that I watched from the beach
now moves like a winged prayer across the drawbridge,
dissolving into the soft darkness,
and I know *something* is in the world.

Falling into birth,
growing like an innocent flower,
barely opening its petals upon earth,
and then leaving.

Parents…family…life…
The drawbridge waits for it to return and closes.

I am pulled into that very soul and for a moment,
know myself beyond this form,
and in the next breath, have forgotten my name.

Current

They walk the stars, seeding the world,
like dream water running,

spilling into paintings and plaintive calls,
to the unknown that abandoned us here.

Spears fly over our heads,
and animals run from under our feet,

until we tire and fall by water's edge,
drinking, knowing something familiar,
as if beginning the way home were here.

Tree

My leaves fell once.
Although no one saw them and they turned to brown,

I was the lucky one,
because the prick of life ignited within my branches.

The sun heated me like a young fire.
I drank the rain like a river,
and for a moment,

I was everything.

Deer in the Water

All things stay where they are.
I do not take them, or move them from their place.
Bones in the woods, relationships, houses,
flowers, coal, trees, and you.

For unto and in, and within,
is the core of a center fixed, and in its place,
still, and silent, from which all outward movement,
and sway, and call emanate.

I only touch and embrace as I can, for a moment,
you and the world, and everything in it,
before you and the world, and everything in it, are gone.

The bones in the woods, the homes on the hill,
the leaves on the ground, and the heart in my chest.

Like sunset, autumn leaves lay.
How beautiful they are in their end,
and how beautiful they were,
as ripe green buds thick with life sap.

And how once,
a dream asked a seed to open itself into life,
and became this tree and this forest,
and these dead leaves at my feet as far as I can see.

Oh life that breaks my heart and frightens me so,
open the dream of my heart,
that I may go forth as a tree without fear
and full with sap, unfurling like a waterfall.

I have lived as a frightened pauper
and am tired of my rags and hunger.

Let me be the river now,
and the sky and the night and the sun.

Oh, bones from my lovely deer,
You have faded away at last,
except for one, lying on the earth.
I am so surprised you are still here, after all these years.

I came to visit you today, and you waited.
Waited for me to find you again.
Oh bone of the deer I saw dead,
half submerged along the banks of the wide-rushing creek.

Oh bones that I visited so often,
watching you become less and less until now.
My visit finds you, one bone only,
from the past of my life, to speak to me and say,

"I am yet alive, whether here or gone,
as are you my child, so choose your dream,
whether here or gone.

And next time, I will not be here for you to remember.
This is my last visit with you, my walking friend."

And so, I say goodbye to my bone in the woods.
The bone that will not be there to remind me
of its life in the form of a beautiful deer,
I saw lying half in the rushing water of the wide creek.

I will leave things as they are.
People, dreams, you, and my memory of a time when feathers,
spirit, and your embrace, were all I knew.

Grace

We have burned.

On fire to pay for this life.
On fire to escape from this life.

I have been on fire long enough.
Let me fall from this burning tree.

And leave the shape of a beautiful leaf,
as gray ash upon the ground.

Dance of Deer and Man

Reading the signs of sky and scent unfolding,
silent steps find her sleeping in earth's grassy hand.
Arcing through air, an arrow finds its home, its red tip still.

She knows a terrible truth and opens her eyes,
falling past her life, and closes them again.

In morning sun she lay.

Bearing her warm weight into the village,
thankful prayers are offered.

Evening cover wraps like leaves and corn within.
Night dreams walk the sky,
and spirit of deer and man bound across the fields.

My Departed Spirit

Nature throws the seeds of antelopes,
buffalo, and eagles into the wind.
They fall into little fires as they touch the ground,
and begin the burning of their soul.

She plants her seeds fanning the world into flame.

We are caught without direction in a river running,
swimming with parents who can barely swim,
clawing our way to shore.

Throwing spears into warm blood.
Wrenching the root of life from ground.
Learning the fear of hunger, and how to kill, for fear of hunger.

From morning's sun, till evening's moon.
From crawling on hands, to walking with cane.

The arm of my fathers bow has long been still.
From the will of my mother's hands,
woven threads of running life hang.
The wake of my children behind the distant waterfall.
Their laughter a memory playing in the stream.

My breath still, like the mountain.
I hear the running paws of earth and feathers in the wind.
The fire of my life has burned to its end.
I have no more will to hunt you.
I have no more will to run from you, who are hunting me.

A leaf is placed on the roof of our hut.
My wife can cook without the rain coming in.
It is good, and of simple things, this day.

Many mornings open like wonder.
Seasons find their heart in the turning pages of trees.
I carry a bowl of water from the river.

Slowly sinking to earth, I am surprised,
at the comfort and warmth of my own blood.
It is unexpected, this spear.

I am burning on the tree.
In ashes, the river of my will.
Like clouds I disappear.

I can see you all.
I want to tell you.
I have no hunger.
I do not have to run.

Nature turns from throwing her seeds into the world.
She walks through me.
Our eyes close together,
one dream, rains upon the earth.

Broken Feather and Walking Leaf

Broken Feather came from the sky and rested on the ground.
Walking Leaf came from the tree and rested on the ground.

When Walking Leaf saw Broken Feather lying on the ground,
she told him that he was born in the air and could fly.

He said he was carried on the wings of the mother bird,
but was hurt and came tumbling down.

Well, "I can't fly, but why can't you?" Walking Leaf asked.
Broken Feather showed how he was broken and bent in
the middle like a V.

Walking Leaf looked at all the birds in the distance and
explained to Broken Feather that he could fly if he moved
forward from his center.

"You mean stick my broken part into the wind?"

And she replied, "Yes, then you will be like the little V's I see
in the distance."

And then the tree, Walking Leaf's mother, said,

"It is only when you lead from the broken place
that you can move again, Broken Feather."

When the beautiful wind came, Broken Feather pointed the
broken part of himself into the wind and he was lifted into
the sky.

He became frightened and called out "Walking Leaf, Walking
Leaf, where are you? I cannot see you for all the other leaves,"
and forgot to point his broken place into the wind and
fell again to earth.

He looked at all the other leaves around him. "Are you Walking Leaf?" he asked, but all he saw were other leaves lying still on the ground. He could not hear her voice anymore.

He waited for her, but she did not come.
Broken Feather tried again. He pointed his broken part into the wind and it lifted him up so high that he felt like he could see the whole world. He called out.

"Walking Leaf, I am flying,
I am up in the wind where I came from.
Where are you Walking Leaf? Where are you?"

He thought he could hear her voice
and even the little crunch sound she made
as she walked and spun across pastures and hilly places.

And sometimes, Walking Leaf would lift up into the wind too, for she learned quickly, and saw how Broken Feather had done it. She found her broken place where she had been torn off from her mother tree and pointed her broken stem into the wind and lifted up towards the sun.

"Wee," she screamed, so amazed that her dreams worked and flew everywhere and showed all the leaves how they didn't have to lay down forever.

Broken Feather felt lonely for his mother bird and for Walking Leaf. He learned to fly very well and would never fall out of the sky if he didn't want to.

One day he landed on the ground after having played in the sun. A sweet and familiar voice called to him.

"Broken Feather? Is that you?"
and Broken Feather turned to Walking Leaf.
"Walking Leaf, is that you?"

"I never got to say thank you.
Thank you for looking at the birds in the distance
and telling me that I was a V like them and could fly."

Walking Leaf said, "I never told you, but after you flew away,
I watched and knew that I could fly too."

The wind blew and they both smiled.

Broken Feather pointed his broken place into the wind,
and Walking Leaf pointed her torn-off stem into the wind,
and as they lifted up into the sky, they knew they could
go wherever they wanted, and that they were free.

Broken Feather laughed in the sky,
and Walking Leaf did, too.

When Blood Was Honey

It is hard to remember,
but once, I saw you simply,
as someone who walked,
much like others your age.

Your gait uneven,
posed a question,
but I never asked why,

and I loved your gait,
and could tell it apart, from anyone else's in the world.

Across the kitchen table, your voice,
of earth, rich, and brown, your eyes,
deep, like warm night.

We watched the leaves change color,
and shared a season together.

Like summer trees filling with ripe full fruit,
I was unable to contain the life of it all,
and joy, tears, and the pulse of my heart,
spilled out like a river.

You flowed back and forth like a gentle wave,
pushing softly against the inside of my skin,
curled inside my heart like a sleeping kitten.

Throughout the day, people and I touched,
radiant, and not knowing why.

Like a young animal taking its first steps of wonder,
ground and wind spoke from behind the hidden veil
of the forest.

I shed my skin and became the tree and the sparrow.
I could no longer see with my old eyes.

I found you in every corner of the garden.
Your heart, like open wings sailing, fell across the world,
and lay like water reeds, bending in the wind.

You are the light and breath of being.
The space where the universe
contracts and expands within your pulsing heart,
its red blood searing with unbearable joy,
life complete and full to bursting,
hailing all creatures and dreams and corralling us away
from the isles of loneliness,
into the formation of the dream of your heart,
until bliss rains down so gently upon us,
that we weep, and are washed away,
and left standing naked, and pure, and refined as gold,
encircled in the arms of your embrace.

From dust, our hands, our blood,
reaching across the boundary of skin.

Walking together along the path of your dream,
the sun did not consider, and neither moon or stars,
as you became the wind.

I held my place between two worlds,
as you rose into the sky like a dragon
fanning its flame over the forgotten fields.

The last chapter closed and the book fell into the sea.
Empty hollows descended and took back the holy gift,
and the knowing of all things ended.

The trees stood mute, the grass plain.
The world had lost its voice. I could not hear it anymore,
nor could I find the dream of spring and birth.

The delicately woven tapestry we knitted together began to
unravel. A tapestry that was beautiful, even sacred.

As a young student I learned how to draw perspective.
One starts with a vanishing point.
Should I have known? That all life and paintings have a
vanishing point?

I watch the glow of my dream,
writhe and twist and struggle to reach for air,
until it lay still, without brightness.

Like a beautiful broken creature,
I pick it up, It's neck limp.
I kneel, and hold it to my chest,
but it does not stir.

There is nothing left,
as the last gentle traces of you fall from my fingers.
The memory of your beautiful heart,
evaporating like morning dew.

Remnant

Sad like slow endings,
a boat abandoned,
dissolves into the sand.

No longer able to cut through life,
as water rushes over.

Ancient Heart

She parted the veil and handed us the warm stars.
We bathed in sunlight and dream.

She waved her hand in the world,
until we remembered who we were.

She left this afternoon to go home.
She was the river that set us free.

Brother Wind

The wind blows,
in the dark starry night,
like a dream of yesterday,
looking for its home.

"Did you make me?" the wind asks.

The dark starry night considers the question.

"What are you looking for Brother Wind?"

"I am looking for who made me,
 why I am blowing through the valleys.
I am looking for the beginning and the end of my life.
I am looking for my name.
I am looking for what happened.
I am looking for why I am in the world."

The Dark Starry Night asked,

"Do you know where you were born Brother Wind?"

"No, I do not know where I was born," the wind answered.

"Do you know what you did Brother Wind?"

"No, I do not know what I did."

"Do you know where you are going Brother Wind?"

"No, I do not know where I am going."

"Do you know why you cry and howl,
and thrust like a mighty wave
covering the world Brother Wind?"

"No I do not know why.
I am carried along on myself as if seeing a dream,
but unable to wake and know myself.

I am only traces of memory
like feathers lost from wings in the sky.

"Tell me what you know Brother Wind."

"I know I am a baby abandoned."

"What was the name they blessed upon your head, little baby?"

"I have no name," the baby in the wind cried,
"I opened my eyes and closed them."

"What did you see Baby In The Wind?"

"I saw my mother looking upon me...
I remember now Dark Starry Night.
I remember her pulling away, and yearning to feel
the warm touch of her heart pressed against my heart."

"I am listening Brother Wind, what do you know?"

"I have clothed myself with flesh again and again to find her,
but always I must return and become the wind."

Morning Dew

Because of our hunger,
we have learned to kill,
and running with the animals,
feel the warmth of skin,

and know that they are so alive,
within their hot and supple hide,
that held their just departed life.

Alone I stand with death and knife.

Its breath released,
the sacred rain,
upon us both, must fall,

dead hump, alone,
on bloody earth,
and I,
yet streaming full.

I worship this sustaining flesh,
and thank the life,
gone from it's breath.

I promise beast, that I will be,
at one within your skin,
and seeing eyes and knowing heart,
and spirit god within,

and walk through trails,
and plains of grass,
and paddle open sea,

to be worthy of,
my earthly breath,
to have taken you, to me.

So roam, my feet, well guided so,
as if my toes were hooves,
along the open sky of day,
your dance within me moves,

me out, to plain and mountainside,
to fetch the early green,
of life, you ate and knew so well,
and hungered for in dream,

of running wild with the wind,
your brothers by your side,
and laying down,
for me at last,
your strength, your grace, and stride.

But now I run like you my guide,
and know the winter frost,
and find the places you once knew,
as home and shelter lost,

to others who have never touched,
your heart and knowing soul,
dissolved as dream into the hills,
before we're ever old.

To run, to run, until my breath,
expires as did yours,
to arrows flight, or kindly yet,
asleep in morning dew.

Sparrow

What a strange thing it is to know that you are becoming
a sparrow. You can see the brown feathers along your skin,
and feel your heart changing into a sparrow heart.
It beats a lot faster. Some of your thoughts are leaving too.

"When is the car payment due?
Will I move into a new apartment?"

And the pain of lost love seems to be gone.

You are thinking about the sky, its air currents,
and the warmth and coolness in different places.

When you look in the mirror, you can see new feathers on
your head where hair used to be, and in this mid-moment
of transformation, it doesn't look too bad.
You figure, it almost looks like a costume you might wear
for Halloween - if you were to go as a bird.

It is for real though, and you really do like these beautiful
feathers, but it feels weird, because things are moving away
from you, things that you wanted, and in some cases,
even loved...
The you, that used to be you, has left...and floated away.

To know, that you only want sparrow things, leaves you
feeling confused. And you try to restart the feelings you
had for people,

and most certainly for the person
you loved with all your heart,
but you can't seem to grasp the feeling anymore.

Eventually, these thoughts leave also, and you begin to notice
little bugs and wonder why they look so delicious.
You used to shoo them outside your room but now you like them.

And as you look around your room, it looks less useful to you.
Why would you need a pen and paper, and what is that foldable
thing on the desk with all those buttons?
The bed looks nice and snuggly but it is so big and empty.

And there is a lamp, yes, I know what that is.
But what are all those things in that open door,
like lots of bed sheets in different shapes hanging on a pole?
I'd fly over to that pole if it weren't so crowded with things.

Oh my, my feet look so cute, I know these feet, wow, they really
can hold onto things.

There is a window, I think that's what it is. I see the trees outside,
and hear birds chirping, and see the sky too. What was I going to
do here? Pay a bill, send an invoice to someone? What is that
anyway? A bill? I'm familiar with all these things here, but I don't
use them. I don't actually know what they are.

The window is open. I never thought this before,
but it occurs to me, that it is plenty big enough,

and then -

I just go.

The Silence of Our Life

I hear your voice in my sleep.

I reach to say your name carefully,
a radiant gift.

Our voices are forgiving,
as two candles in the dark.

In the two names, our union.

We are unmarked, unformed and blank,
willing to know each other,

and in the same moment,
of having known each other.

I wake,
having heard your voice and my voice together,
as if our spirits were communing,
apart from the us that we are in our separate lives.

Tear

You are in a boat looking out to sea.

The rope,
no longer in my hand.
I cannot understand this moment,

too far to reach and pull back,

I can still see the loose strands,
as you drift away.

The Galaxy

I guess we're made to look straight ahead.
We don't look up much,
sky, stars at night -

Always thankin' bout the next meal,
or the next deal, and willin' to fight for it too,
got to keep looking straight ahead.
That's how we're made.

So…I don't know what's wrong with me,
but I keep lookin' up.

All those stars at night… d'you know the sun's a star?

Our own star right here, come round every day,
make a whole world full o' grass…kids runnin',
and hard gray factories, shaping metal into cars,
and bombs and killing each other.

Just can't fit it in my head sometimes.
So I look up thankin',
It'll come to me.

One time,
I just made it all up.

I went up there,
stirred them stars real good,
just like I's in the kitchen.
Then I spread 'em out all over,
like I's a farmer, spread 'em out over the whole field.

Called it somethin' - galaxy...there you go.
They liked that name. Slapped it on some car way back.
Had white walls, all shiny like...fancy dashboard,
galaxy... like you in outer space,
like you knowed everythin' driving that car down the road.
Nah, couldn't top that...well, fer a minute anyway.

Gone now - it's alright, just like everythin'.

My kids' blowed some bubbles.
I's laying on the grass jus' looking up,
like I say, we all don't look up much,
and they was laughin'.

I saw all them bubbles float by,
thought, what if you was in one of 'em?
Like them stars you don't know nothin' 'bout,
but looking close, like right here,
it's the God dang earth with all o' everythin'.

Maybe there's a bubble with Emma 'bout to have her baby,
an' one with Rick holdin' his M16,
bout to blow someone's head off, ...
and a' course, one with us on grandma's porch,
where we is right now...

I'd hold 'em all, fix the broke ones, maybe smile some,
but you know the deal,
ain't but a few seconds and they gone.

So anyway, I take this old Galaxy out o' the junkyard,
fix her up good. Don't know why,
just something underneath pushing...

I bring her back from the dead, all shiny like.
I figure, maybe the car God 'ill fix me up good when it's time.

I git some gas and a rough old cowboy come over,
stands a ways off staring,
has to break through his own hardened crust I guess.
Somethin' 'bout the car, hooked him good.
He stares like he's a lookin' at his whole life,
and countin' everythan' that ever happened,
from the front bumper to the back.

"Just finished this morning... maiden voyage," I said.

Two piercing blue eyes, look like ice water,
as if he assessing the price of cattle.

"Bill," he said.
The man had some rough hands.
"Steve," I said.

He coughed, and held up his palm in a gesture of
- wait a minute- shaking his head with the cough.

Wiped his mouth on his faded denim jacket, took a breath.
The gas station man helped a woman at the pump.
Some bird like to take my head off, flit so close.

"Used to have that car...well, one just like it..." he said.

"That your truck?" I asked.

"Yeeaah," he drawled, "been a while."

"Been a while what?" I asked.

"Since I rightly fixed her up, but this here," looking at the
Galaxy, "You done right."

Some geese flew over honkin',
further they git, sound more like cryin'.
He look at the car 'gain, gits to talking.

"My date...in this car right here... 'came the love of my life,
our kids squeezing in the back seat,
trips to Ma and Pa's,
spilling ketchup and fries everywhere,
laughing till their socks fell off...the stain finally come out -
- and my kids cryin' when I had to git a new car...
so many memories in this one.

They stood 'round and waved 'Bye Galaxy,' and I beeped the horn
so was like the car saying goodbye back, all the way down the road."

But then - he stopped - had to catch his breath.
"Oh, my God" he said, some crazy look on his face.

"You ok?" I asked.

He stared, kinda crushed in like...
"What color was your car 'fore you fixed it?" he asked.

"Holy shit"..............."Light Blue" I said.

"Jesus..."

I never told no one, towed that old wreck home, in the trunk,
someone scratched somethin' inside - I's mad as a mule,
what stupid fool done that, but then I looked - was a heart,
and inside it said...

- I love you Jenny -

"Oh my God," I wondered, is this the old cowboy that done that?

Hell, I just come in to git some gas.

I asked him again. "You alright now?"

He shook his head like a weak old thang,
but his voice came out good.

"Yeeaah - I'm fine."

I walked over to the trunk,
put the key in, and 'fore I turned it, I said, "Alright," cause I knew
his life 'bout to spill right out.

Morning lit up them words.

He didn't say nothin'.

"Go ahead," I said.

He stared, moved his hand close, and touched 'em, like her face,
and said "Jenny…"

"Hey sweetie," he smiled, touched her name again.
Something right grabbed my insides.
I had to look at the ground and swallow hard.

Darlin', you please hand me the sugar, and your hands touched,
and you looked at each other, and kids ran up the hill in summer
screaming, their kites crazy high, and breakfast pancakes,
the kitchen full of butter sizzling in the pan,
and coffee steaming out hot like when she poured it in yer cup,
and "Don't forget to heat the syrup!"

And "I want chocolate chips in mine!" and holding hands, saying
"Thank you God, for Mommy and Sean and Jane... and pancakes!
Amen!" and everybody laughed so hard they cried, and you said...
"I want the biggest one! 'cause I'm the boss!"

He just dropped his head, hung there, like he wasn't no one.

She's there, talking quiet, running through.

I heard it, don't know what she was saying,
but it was something like...

"I love you Billy."

Ain't no words to figure.
Th'other side open wide as a field, you can't see nothing,
but everything is there...can't reckon if your breathin'.

Gas pump clicked off.
This moment was done...

Pulled himself up...
He was with her, took a breath, coughed, gestured with his head.

"I put this here, so she'd see it, every time she opened the trunk."

"I couldn't erase it," I said.

"Naw, you can't never erase that," he said, and looked at the ground.

I waited, a little voice in my head said, "Put the gas handle back on
the pump." I did.

The old cowboy closed the trunk slow, as if there was some
sort of holy thang in there. He stepped away and looked up.

Two birds flew above the trees, we watched 'em trail out till
we couldn't see 'em no more.

He was different now. Silent, like some cowboy who knows
'bout the river and how it run. 'Bout birthin' calf in the field,
and putting 'em down when it's time.

"You gotta be gentle, when you clutch into first gear with
this baby."

"I know." I said,

"And you don't want to take a turn hard or she'll roll like a barrel."

I shook my head yes.

"And you want to keep a good check on the distributor timing,
but sounds like she's running fine."

"She is." I answered.

"All right then," he said. "You take care of her now."

He looked at me, and then the car.

"I hope you're as lucky as I was."

I held back a wave of something.
He shook my hand, his rough palm
pressing the memory of his life into mine.

And said, "Yeeah, that's about right."

He stepped back a bit, looked again.

"Now you get outta here, okay?"

I said, "You bet," and felt I was leaving my father and my
brother, that I was the shining bubble that would break and
never come back.

I kept thinking of what this man named Bill looked like,
when he saw the scratches in the trunk of this old Galaxy.
That he wanted somethin' so bad, that it come to him again.

How it come to be then, that his road come this way?
Way down, in the water o' everything,
somethin' deep musta moved, brought me here,
and then of course, I look up, I always do…

And the farmer opens the sluice again, raining the dream of
Bill's life all over me, pouring out the steering wheel and the
dashboard, and I remember…

the date that became the love of his life, his kids squeezing in the
back seat, trips to Ma and Pa's, spilling ketchup and fries
everywhere laughing, and how the stain finally come out,
and the kids cryin' when he had to git a new car,
an' stood 'round waving,

"Bye Galaxy,"

and he beeped the horn,
so was like the car saying goodbye back, all the way down the road.

I'm in Bill's car now, with his wife and kids driving away,
and will never see him again.

I hear the voice of his wife Jenny, she calls my name.

"Steven…Thank you…"

I burst out in tears, and pull over. I set there in the car till
the sun melts our lives into a river, and somehow, a smile come to
my face, and I put the old Galaxy in gear, and press on the gas.

I guess we're made to look straight ahead.
We don't look up much, the sky, stars at night -

Always thankin' bout the next meal,
or the next deal, and willin' to fight for it too,
got to keep looking straight ahead.

That's how we're made.
So...I don't know what's wrong with me,
but I keep lookin' up.

Heart of Tree

I am cold bones and cool shade
born on spring grass.

I welcomed your embrace.
Your spirit poured into my branches.

My children floated away.
Your dreams and theirs mixed together.

Paintings upon the earth.
The whisper of your life.

Her Way Home

Upon the water, a leaf.

One foot in the current of the river,
and one on the sandy sun drawn whisper.

Lost in wonder,
searching through light and trees.

A hand opens to release the arrow,
finding the warm ocean of her heart.
She lays herself down and paints her last breath.

The soft door behind her eye opens.
Her life passes through like a wave of the forest.

Glowing with the god of light,
inner wings spread like the hidden symbol of creation.

Her heart, for my breath.

The Gate of the Universe

I sit in the kitchen and look across the table.
There is an empty chair on the other side,
where I used to talk with you.

When dreams passed through like a soft waves.

The sun opened the window then,
and there was nothing sweeter than your soft slippers
shushing across the floor.

Like the buds of young flowers in the fresh pull of spring,
you bloomed into a new dream every day.

Over and over you bloomed, until I surrendered, and the blood
of my life became translucent and lifted me into the sky.

The blood of your life, was like sun in your veins,
and lit the world, and opened the gates of the universe,
until its light spilled into the earth.

The universe felt it's light pouring into the world
and saw you holding the heavy gates open.

"And who is this?" the Universe asked.

"You know who I am, now help me hold these gates open."

The Universe laughed. "Those gates look very heavy my dear,
are you sure you have the strength to hold them?"

You became angry, "You're the one who told me to open them
in the first place! Why are you not helping me? I can't hold
them open by myself!"

The Universe laughed and said,
"More than anything, you are my heart,"
and froze the gates open with the grace of wheat
bending in the field.

As you let go of the heavy gates your last breath faded,
and you fell to earth.

We never knew you were saying goodbye,
and held our hands open to catch you from so high above,
but you fell like rain upon our skin and eyes.

Light poured from the gates and reached into the forests and
the deep ocean, and every creature knew, an angel had opened
the heart of the universe.

I stir now, in the deep night alone, and walk through a lonely
dream upon the silent desert, hoping that somehow you have
not left us forever.

But breaking anchor from heavens shore, a familiar angel rows
an old wooden boat across the universe into the parting veil of
earth...

From across the barren desert of my dream, I hear your voice.
I wake and look into the night, but cannot see anything except
the outline of trees.

Turning back into the room, I can almost hear your step,
as if you had come in through the window.

You are here.

Stars and flowers rain from the ceiling and feathers of light
become my wings.
Your arms hold me in the warmest embrace I have ever known,
and we are in the kitchen again.

I look across the table…
…to the chair on the other side, and now, it is not empty,
you are sitting there, and I talk with you.

Stars pour out of your eyes and fill the kitchen with little flowers,
and soft arcs of fire float off your skin, like feathers of light
blowing up to heaven.

I talk with you and it feels like the wind of the universe,
and you look back, and smile, the sun burning from
within your heart.

Three Spirits

What a struggle it is,
to carry the three of myself around...
and to live with them all.

I wish I could just drop the two of them off...
that have taken up residence,
and will not leave-

There is really only me,
the real one... right here... inside,
and I love you, and you, and you.

But this other one,
keeps telling the real me
to worry about life and money,
and never stops talking.

As if that wasn't enough to drive me crazy,
there's another me that is pretty much grown up,

and gets tired,
and has pains,
and runs out of energy,
and is tempted by dessert and beautiful things.

I try so hard to just be the real one,
but the other two are almost always in the way.

Especially, when I try to talk with anyone,
the thinking version screws things up right away,
and the physical version poses,
and tries to communicate its own agenda.

I'd slap myself five times a day,
if that would get rid of the silliness
these other two bring along with themselves,

but I've tried and my body just says-

"Ouch, that hurts,"

and my non-stop talking self says-

"You need me, you'll screw up if I don't worry for you!"

Thank God for stillness... and meditation...
at least then I have the hope,
that for a little while,
the other two will leave me alone.

The Wake of Our Life

Walking through the weather of this world,
fading into shivering crackly brown,
our sails blow like ghosts in the wind.

Shifting from inside to out along the plains and fields,
like a stone thrown from starry birth,
into the dry bony hand on cane,
holding the whisper of goodbye.

Waking from a Thousand Years

Am I called to the baby's heart
or to the seeds in the field?
To the seagull, or the running deer?
To be male or female?
To be green as grass, or gray like the trunk of a tree?

What will I become as I move above the earth?
My left hand has swept the land clean,
my right hand rains with life and spring.

Brown Leaves Never Come Back to Green

She pressed them clothespins tight so them sheets ain't snap
off the wind like feathers flyin',
and washed her hands at the pump one at a time 'cause to
pump with one of 'em.

White, like the flag o' surrender blowin', cleaned out o' the hard
slept husband, laid down in the field.

Sun and stones won that battle.
His hands pulling out the ground all she gave.

Good wife she was, draggin' him out the furrows,
told him he's everything.

"Ain't going nowhere woman," he said.

But he look at her, like to sayin' goodbye twenty time.

"I'll smack you good if you don't git up," she said.

He smiled the best one he had. "You better woman, I wouldn't
'spect nothin' less."

Right then it broke - she threw herself on top of his shirt with
the smell of the field an' farm,

and that heart was a beating one....of the whole world.

Like the two arms a his still holding her,
he knowed it was this way -

'Tween here and yesterday was forever,
like that book yer holdin', when you fell asleep, and jus' woke
with yer finger stuck in the last page.

It's coming, so might as well git in it now.

She put her head on his shoulder and they never talked so loud
without talkin'
What like to words they were - like the sun burning.

"John...   Jenny..."

...never saw a blade of grass that close,

and then I remembered, and saw my husband laying there,
like the most beautiful thing I ever saw,

and the sun lit his beautiful face,
so I could see it good.

Winter Night

Deep dark winter night,
specks of ice fall and sing,
against the window from such great height,
as little bells that ring.

From unknown places in the wind,
each jewel visits sweet,
and tapping on the window pane,
good friend that I should meet.

But before I can wave back and smile,
they tap and dance away,
and make a magic melody,
that only they can play.

I hear the heart of all of them,
in silent turn of earth,
between the dark and day of life,
a chorus full of mirth.

So pure their touch,
their spirits pass, through window's glass, unseen,
they only live, to call out once,
and fall into my dream.

They dance along with blood of heart,
and sing the ancient song,
of winter's sparkling night again,
forgotten for so long.

Last Breath

Who was I?
Who were we all?

Every word ever spoken,
now water in the stream,
and wind gentle against the leaves.

Joe's Diner

Without our guide there was no path,
and since none of us knew for sure,
we all went our own way and found pebbles and plants by the
side of the road, and little animals, and then the sky, open wide,
until we started to think, that maybe we understood something.

And taking a step from kiddie jammies into business suits and
finally into the earth, we look down and smile, because we all
ended up at Joe's diner.

I'm sitting in a booth near the window and he asks from behind
the counter,

"What do you want?" and I say, "Pancakes!"

He leans in.

"Do you want the sweet syrup of life? …of buttery maple hot
and steaming, or do you want the bitter black coffee and burnt
dry toast?"

I'm taken aback that he would ask that, but before I can answer,
an unshaven man in a black leather jacket sits down in the booth
with me and says, "Yeah, I'll take that, and spit in the coffee too."

"You want some venom?" old Joe asks knowingly.

"Oh yeah, like right from the snake tooth."

"Oh, don't listen to him," the waitress chimes in, and pours my
coffee. She smiles and says, "Your pancakes will be right up."

"Hey sweetie," the man says. "How 'bout a cup for me too?"
"You'll get yours soon enough," she says, and walks away with
the pot in her hand.
I look out the window and see the Andromeda galaxy swirling
and know we are the Gods of the universe planting our seeds.
We're moving so slow that we can see a thousand years moving
in real time.

"Come on, wadd'ya really want?" old Joe asks my new
companion.

"Oh all right," the man says. "If you really wanna know,
I'm here to take you all."

"All right," Joe says, and pulls out a shotgun and fires.

There are stars glowing on my shirt like little diamonds, like
tiny lives blinking, and I instinctively go to brush them off,
thinking, "Oh my God, he's all over me," but then I realize,
gruff as he was, he was only stars. And Joe smiles and says,
"Yup, only stars, but you know, there's no need to be nasty.
We all come into the diner the same way."

I'm scared and not scared. The stars melt into my skin through
my shirt and they feel warm and wonderful and I understand he
just got off on the wrong side of things.

The waitress brings my pancakes out and I know I'm really
home. Joe cracks some eggs in the pan. As he flips them up in
the air, I see they are not eggs at all, but little stars floating up
and falling on the counter and on my shirt and then I realize,
"Oh, that is all we ever were," and I look at Joe, and he smiles.

Morning Mist

A petal floats down the river.
Wind lays upon your skin.

Water talks with the riverbank
and pours into the open field of your heart.

Flowers push themselves into the sea of blue air.

A fish swims to welcome you.
Deer run in the waving straw.

Sum of Breath

Dissolving into air, floating up to sky, remembering all
the lives, and then your own, the regrets...the hurt others
put upon you, the not understanding why, the aches,

the moment of unexplained laughter...

and the quiet spaces in the busy life,
where something spoke for a moment,

...and you knew...

and thought you would remember, as life started up again,
but forgot over and over, until it drifted away in the wind,

and further up now, the world so round...
you wonder, if you were anyone at all.

The Little Bird

The Little Bird saw a man with a broom sweeping the dust
off the sidewalk into the street. He moved with a flowing dance
and the broom danced with him, and bits of dust
swirled into a little cloud.

People walked by steering clear of the dusty cloud and the
man stopped sweeping, and the cloud settled to the ground.

The man turned on a hose, and stars and rivers ran glossy into
little waterfalls over the curb into the street and reflections of
sun played shiny there.

The Little Bird asked the man why he was sweeping all the stars
and sparkly rivers. The man looked around as if he
heard his name.

The City walked with bags on shoulders and pocketbooks
dangling and backpacks and cigarettes and coffee.

The Little Bird flew from building to building, feeling pulled
by every ledge looking for home. It was tiring, and the
Little Bird stopped on the street and looked at all the feet.

"What do you have to give me, little Sparrow?" a man asked.
The Little Bird looked up and wondered why the giant was
standing there.

The man said, "Mhff bwantifuff wawa?" The man was
smiling and asked again, "Mhff bwantifuff wawa?"

There was a sparkle in the gutter.
"Oh, the lake!" ...and it was good to take a bath.

The man sweeping the stars came to sweep away the lake too,
his brushy brush singing "Sweep sweep," and the Little Bird
was glad for the bath and hopped a few feet away.

With one hand clasped to the warm flesh of his mother's
hand and his other hand free to wiggle in the air,
a little boy pointed and said, "Mommy, look at the Little Bird."

"Why are you in the street Little Bird?" he asked.

Suddenly, the little boy and the Little Bird were in a bubble.
It was very quiet. Everything else was like a movie outside.
But it was slow and hardly moving at all, so there was no rush.

They had tea together.

"What is this?" the little boy asked.

"It is everything," said the Little Bird.

"I'm confused," admitted the little boy.

"You won't be confused," said the Little Bird.

"Really?" asked the little boy.

"Soon you will know…"

And the little boy's mother took his hand and said,
"Come on, leave the Little Bird alone," and pulled him away.

She walked with wings on top, brown, flapping in the wind.

Wings flapped on everyone's head when the wind blew,
but they never left the ground. Big walking birds they must be.

Deep in the night, the Little Bird dreamt of sparkles like rain
and took a bath in the sparkly water and sang like little bells.

The little boy dreamt too. He was flying with the Little Bird.
They both perched on a tree and saw a man walking with his
briefcase. He looked like he was really going somewhere.

"Where are you going?" The little boy asked.

But the man with the briefcase only heard a bird chirping.
He looked up for a moment, and remembered something
he may have lost, not like a pen or a book, but one of his pasts.
He was on top of a mountain, he could see something…but he
remembered he had no time and walked down the street.

A mommy was pushing a baby stroller. The little boy tweeted,

"Mommy, where are you going?"

She looked up and remembered she was having the best moment
of her life. "Hello Little Bird!" she smiled. The wind suddenly
blew leaves all over, and mommy picked up her baby and sang
"Weeeeee!" and danced in the swirling leaves.

The little boy turned to the Little Bird in his dream
and asked "Why are you so quiet?"
The Little Bird sounded deep like the great knowing and said
"Life has already decided." And faded away.

When the little boy woke up, he remembered flying with the
Little Bird and then snuggled under the covers to make the
dream come back.

But the dream did not come back. He rubbed his eyes and
opened the window.

So many birds were chirping that it sounded like a party. Then he remembered the fairy tale from the warm covery snuggle of blanket and mommy close. She had read the last line of the story:

"From the top of the mountain, he could see the whole world." And had closed the book with a kiss. He felt like sunny wiggles and outside his window the school of the birds had begun.

"I am going to teach you some magic today," the teacher of the birds explained. "We are little birds and cannot sail upon the wind like our brothers, our wings are small and we must flap flap flap to keep flying, but today I want you to do something different, I want you to close your eyes, and allow yourself to fall with your little wings open, no flapping, just keep your wings stretched out to see what happens." Many little beaks and eyes looked up and wondered like lost clouds, but the Little Bird felt like the sun, warm and yellow like a dream.

He flew as high as he could, held his wings open, and closed his eyes.

He felt the wind alongside all his feathers and it was like the wind was Somebody. As if the wind had invisible wings pressing against his own. He began to fall to earth, but something else began to happen too. He began to hear the wind's thoughts, and for the first time ever, realized the wind was his brother and had held him up since he first fluttered out of his nest.

"Hi Brother Wind!" He chirped,

and the wind said, "Hi Little Bird!"

The Little Bird asked "Brother Wind, do you ever sleep?"

And the wind answered, "My still part is sleeping and my windy part is awake, we trade off when I get tired of blowing."

"My teacher said to fall with open wings,
"chirped the Little Bird,

and the wind said, "Fly up high again, and listen."

So The Little Bird flew up high, and held his wings open.
He closed his eyes and let himself fall to earth.
He forgot about bird class, looking for home, and food.
He felt like he was the wind.

He could hear everything in the world, the lion roaring and the fish breaking the surface of the water, the child crying for its mother, and then, he heard the voice of his own mother.

He opened his eyes and flap flap flapped in time to land on a tall tree and all the leaves clapped "Yay!" for the little bird, and the Little Bird said, "Thank you!" to the tree and to the wind.
After the leaves stopped clapping, he heard the wind whisper,
"I am here forever."

He had never tried to go for long without flapping, and now he learned what he'd always taken for granted,
that his flapping wings were everything.

When he allowed himself to fall, he understood that his life could end. Suddenly, he saw magic in everything.
The sky had its clouds, the trees had their leaves,
and he had his wings!

He couldn't wait to go to bird class and wondered what his teacher would say.

The little boy walked into the kitchen with the covers on his head. His mommy asked, "Are you the blanket monster?" He roared with his arms sticking out from under the blanket and he couldn't see so he bumped into things. "May I talk with the blanket monster?" Mommy asked again. He pulled the blanket off his head and said "Hello, Mommy!" and smiled proudly for hiding the monster.

"What would you like to do today?" she asked.

"I want to go to the park and get ice cream and play with my friends."

"I think we can do that," she said and began to make breakfast. She made him a pancake and an egg and he said the egg was yucky because it broke and spilled out.
Mommy said, "I'm so happy you broke the egg because now all the good fish can swim out."

"I'm a good fish," he said, and made believe he was a fish monster and roared. He walked to his mommy and hugged her legs and she picked him up and they drove to the park and she bought him ice cream.

"What swims in ice cream Mommy?" he asked, licking the sweet cold softness. Mommy didn't know what swam in ice cream, so she looked at the little boy, and had one thought;
"It is a dream you are my son."

The Little Bird was flying in the park because there was always something to eat there. He remembered, "Close my eyes, and sail with open wing," and fell from the sky. Just before touching the ground, he flapped his little wings and swirled up.

The little boy looked up with ice cream on his face and cried, "Mommy, it's the Little Bird!" The Little Bird had landed on a rock, and was standing on one leg.

The little boy looked at his mommy. She smiled and said,
"Walk slowly, don't scare him away."
She wiped the ice cream from his mouth and he handed her
the cone.

He tiptoed toward the Little Bird. She held the ice cream
thinking; "I'd better eat it so it doesn't drip all over my hand
and clothes." She closed her eyes to go into the sweet taste
and wondered, "What swims in ice cream?"

The little boy came close to the Little Bird and a bubble
shined around them and the grownups disappeared.
Inside the bubble was something he had never seen.
A soft chair made of feathers.

The Little Bird unfolded his other leg and walked over to
the chair and nestled in. He looked funny in the feathery
chair, like a Little Bird king. The little boy sat on the rock
and wondered if maybe he was the king of birds.
But he did not ask that.

"Do you always close your eyes?" the little boy asked.

"Yes, and one day I will not open them again."

The Little Bird asked, "Is the warm snuggle...forever?"

And the little boy said "Yes."

The Little Bird flitted out of the feather chair and was gone.
He couldn't help himself - all the other birds were so springy
and jumpy. He flew to them and jumped and sprang and
chirped.

A man put a hot dog on a bun and gave it away.
A man gave him something back, and they said thank you.

The Little Bird was eating food that fell near big feet and the men would talk to the birds and say, "Mhff bwantifuff wawa".

The Little Bird filled his belly and chirped for the little boy, but the little boy did not come.

There was no bubble or tea and the Little Bird felt like he was only half. The wind rang the bell of his name and he swirled up into the sky.

The little boy went to his mommy.

"Mommy?"

"Yes sweetie?"

"Where is the Little Bird?"

"He will come whenever you call."

"Oh."

And so, the little boy went back to the rock and called.
He really just whispered …"Little Bird"… and the Little Bird flew back to the rock. The bubble formed around them and everything on the outside slowed down. A few soft muffled sounds filtered through.

There were only three things inside the bubble, a feather chair, a little boy, and a Little Bird. After a moment of silence the little boy asked, "May I sit in the feather chair?"
The Little Bird paused, and then said, "Yes."

The feather chair was soft and the little boy felt tickled inside, like he was the good fish and wanted to roar.

"Why do you stand on one leg, Little Bird?"

"Wouldn't you like some tea first?" the Little Bird inquired.

"Oh yes!" the little boy answered.

They had tea together. The little boy forgot his question and thought how nice tea was.

"What is my name?" the Little Bird asked.

The little boy knew it was "Bird on One Leg" but he did not say it out loud.

"Do you like the feathery chair?" the Little Bird asked.

"I love the feathery chair!" the little boy exclaimed, "It makes me feel like I am a bird."

"Are you a bird? I thought you were a little boy?"

And the little boy looked down and saw that he had grown wings and how feathery nice they were and got so excited that he flitted away.

The Little Bird thought, "I know your name too, little boy."

And The Little Bird decided to close his eyes and dream. The little boy's mother came to him in the dream and even though he was a bird, she tucked him in all snuggly, and read the bedtime story:

"From the top of the mountain he could see the whole world."

"I'm here mom!" the little boy chirped, but his mom kept calling for him, even though he was flying right in front of her. She made all these funny noises and kept searching for something she had lost.

He flew to her feet and sang a beautiful song. He flitted up by her translucent eyes and only then noticed, that she was the night and the stars. Then he remembered that she was his mom too and chirped as loud as he could, "Tweet tweet tweeeeeeeeet!" She looked at him and knew something wonderful, but then worried again and looked around as if her heart was gone, and she didn't know how to breathe without a heart.

He flew back, and as his little bird legs touched the rock, the bubble formed around them again.

The Little Bird was standing on one leg dreaming about snuggly covers and mommy's warm voice telling a story about the mountain. He opened one eye and then the other and shook his head.

The little boy sat in the feathery chair.

There was a little piece of the warm ocean still swirling inside the Little Bird and he cried a tear. He said, "I love you Little Boy." And the little boy in the feathery chair said, "I love you too Little Bird." He walked over to the Little Bird and sat down on the rock next to him. His wings had disappeared. He was a little boy again.

"I guess I should go to my mommy," the little boy said.
"Did you see the star?" The Little Bird asked.
"I saw them all," The little boy said, and then he asked, "What is my name?"

The Little Bird said, "Would you like some tea?" and the little boy said, "I think that is a funny name." And they both laughed. It was a chirpy wiggle laugh and it was so warm that the shiny bubble almost melted.

A few people looked over at a rock and saw a boy, and a little bird hopping, and wished they had the same innocence.

Mommy saw her little boy on the rock, and her heart came back and she could breathe again, and seeing the Little Bird, decided not to wash them away in the bursting dam of her emotion. She just watched her little son and the Little Bird, and remembered when she talked with a little bird once and asked it to be still so she could draw it with a crayon.

The little boy looked through the bubble and could see his mommy. She was waving and smiling. He waved to her and thought how much he loved her and snuggly covers and bedtime stories.

He walked over to the feathery Little Bird chair and looked at it for a long time, and sat down.

He closed his eyes and felt the soft feathery beauty form through his arms and the call of the sky pulled him up to the sun. He flew and flew, and then… closed his eyes, and descending with open wings, disappeared into the breath of the wind.

Little Wing

You step over the creek light as fine china balanced on its
sweetly fragile edge.

I feel the warm touch of life within your gentle hand
as I reach to steady you just barely.

You, little butterfly, dance from stone to stone
playing catch in the cuddling air.

Looking again, I see through human eyes that it is you still,
balancing and laughing, drinking in the day,

your eyes a mirror of the light of dreams.

Summer Kite

How like dream you played upon my hand,
like summer sand welcome in the blue water touch of day,
along the breezy air, lightly up and away, kites taut and pull,
of hands stringy scrape and reel spinning, home not so far,

at tables recounting, the brightness,
like magical dreams become real,
and sad beddy bye time when all things stop and still,
and mothers leaning over, kiss on forehead final,
to bed and closing eyes and dreams like puppies jumping.

Trying one corner, and then another, rushing up into the sky,
finding the kites that flew before,
swirling back down into your feet,
finding legs and little hands holding.

Oh yes, this is the day I had today, and having touched to be sure,
rushes off, to find new meaning, as if a moments pause,
would be a chain, and the end of brimming over.

And parents call, dogs licking faces, your early morning room again,
and wonder what you are, knowing something like a little pin,
and then everything… before you can breathe, the weight of your
new arms and legs and head on the pillow, scream with enthusiasm,
to jump away from the sleep that held you captive.

And the lightly go lucky wisp of dream flits past like a quickly
flapping bird, and wonder stops your step, on the way to the
bathroom to pee, and floods your eyes, the day of kite, and beach,
and sand and dream, and brush your teeth, all birdies having found
their two trees, and likewise your spurt and sprout, the one of day
and wow and wonder… and the night of dream, like a wild movie
flying and diving.

Like a needle stitching your little *boo!* life, reckless and laughing.

Tears of the Forest

The path lay hidden in the open heart of falls welcoming color.
A thunderous rain had faded into soft balmy air.
In the stillness that followed, I surrendered.

The rocks and straw grasses reached out and spoke.
Birds chirped, sparkling like little gems,
and the wind rocked the forest back and forth,
like a loving parent holding it's dearest child.

For a moment I remembered,
a lifetimes worth of unresolved questions,
and in that same moment, they all drifted away.

The waves in my blood sensed the call of their ancient birth,
and soft air touched skin, speaking in the language of the wind.

Two rivers flowed.
The blood of ancient knowing,
and wind, breathing life into the world.
And as the wind blew,
the forest spoke, with a great chattering rustle.

Every flower, leaf, and insect breathed,
under the airy blanket of open sky.
The wind rested, and gray light reigned.

Impressions of the forest began to unfold.
The rocks, holding the record of fire and creation.
The sky, holding the record of dreams.
And the straw field, holding the record of all our prayers.

Prayers for rain to fall, for the birth of a child,
for sickness to be healed, and for suffering to end.
A few birds called out. We breathed together.

Their short breaths...my longer breaths.
Their feathered wings...my fingered hands.
Our feathers and skin. Our sun and moon.

It was time to kneel before the hearth of earth,
to thank the Gods and Goddesses,
and the smallest blade of grass.
It was time, to cry the rivers of goodbye.

The clouds parted and yellow brightness flooded the field.
Tall grasses swayed lazily, unaware of their beauty.
In harmony with the rites of autumn, I too will part,
and rest with leaves upon the earth.

Of birth and death, of joy and sorrow.
All things exist together as one,
and remembering becomes forgetting,
and forgetting becomes remembering.

As the harvest of years turn lives under the soil
to be born again, I will reach for you like a lost river,
looking for its way home.

I held the sheen of sharp silver as it found its place,
and recalled the union of our spirits
until the flood of our ocean spilled over.

Silent tears guided the edge, as I etched the memory of life's red
glow over my heart. You seared apart the prison,
and burned away the dross.

The wind began to blow like thunder.
The brown earth and the straw colored grass held out their arms.
High above the mountain in the sun of heart and sky,
I felt your wing brush through like sacred wind.
I was holding you lightly, like a tiny bird innocent and fragile.

I was holding light and life itself.
I was protecting the grace within grace as the wind from your hand.
Falling through the suspension of the world,
the last of your heart ran along the edge of my breath.
I heard a distant voice in the sky struggling to say the word...

"Goodbye."

The fertile ground hummed its song of earth,
and soft leaves rained their gentle brushstrokes of solace.
I was unwilling to move from that space and moment in time,
...but the day had to end.

The light began to alter its color, and the wind began to cool,
and a sense of season, time, and cycles began to speak,
as deeply as the voices of the forgotten tribes.

Like a tiny drop of rain, preceding a greater rain that is to come,
a drop of night fell from the sky,
and the wind whispered with the rumbling earth.

"Between life and death, you must remain."

I walked through the fallen leaves and heard their last prayer,
that even in parting from their mother tree, there is beauty.
And though I cannot understand it, and only shed black tears,
there is beauty in parting from you, my angel.

I am with every soul praying in the fields

...as are you.

The fire burns, as all life burns, beautiful, forever.

To Know

One day I will wake with no children,
I will wake with no wife by my side,
I will wake with no friends to remember,
I will wake with parents long gone,
One day, I will wake alone.

I will stand high above the earth,
and know who I am.

Sea of Wind

Leaves sing their feathery softness,
dancing in the grace of day.

Deer float like flower petals in the wind,
soft arches weightless over tall grass.

White mountains drift over the world,
old wisdom protecting the sky.

Memoir: Stepfather

For a moment, I could not see, hear, think, smell, or
understand anything. I was suspended in an increment of
time where my brain was awash in chemicals and could not
keep up with the speed of the event. As if in another world,
my consciousness left and I was suspended, as if life was
simply shut off for a moment. That was it. Life had stopped
so completely that my memory was blank. There was nothing
to record, nothing to remember, only the beginning and exit
from being suspended, that I remember.

There was accusation, anger. Not mine. Someone else's.
I remember my brother sitting next to me, happy at the
dinner table. Its broad distance between us and the offender.
The gold yellow kingly paint on the close walls of the dining
room, the spectacularly large deep rich and beautifully carved
piece of furniture that held the silver and dinner finery.
The two wooden lions supporting the upper shelf, their
expressions, committed to angry protection. The shelf
lined with platters of various artistic expression.

Wine found itself a constant at this table, as well as our dog
Tie, and my mother and stepfather across from us, close, and
distant as the stars.

So many times he had told us, this man we called Tom, how
to hold the fork so that the tip of ones finger pressed near the
back where the tongs of the fork curved and arched into
a gentle and giving shape. We had been talking or laughing,
or just bored, or tired, or silly. How many faces and
personalities can you bring to the dining room table as a nine
year old?

Sometimes we would feed the dog, Rick and I. We'd hide the
food in our napkin and drop it on the beautiful Oriental rug,
and give out a silent call, for Tie to come to our aid.

86

Tie had to learn our language. We would wish our thoughts to him. Then he would come, small, long haired, and looking like a caterpillar, his hair covering both eyes. He learned our cues, gestures from our hands and feet done in silent space.

My brother and I worked our secret alongside each other, our chairs close.

We would hear Tie eating and tried to reach him with our mind telling him to eat more quietly. He was usually quiet, but sometimes he would masticate without regard for the secrecy that we had entrusted him with.

My brother and I knew it could be either one of us. It could come at anytime. It was usually delivered with such practiced quickness that it seemed impossible. How could this stinging, spreading across my face like fire, come out of nowhere?

It came, with the kind of irregularity that kept Rick and myself in a young Zen like acceptance. Acceptance of a sharp hard hand knocking the present out of our heads until we cried.

We would learn. We did learn. Like breathing and bathing, there was the edge of not knowing at the table. We learned to rest on that edge in controlled balance until the malevolent wind blew, choosing one of us.

The hand that moved so quick was attached to this man who was continually replenished from the winds of the past.

They would go searching for generations and eons, finding channels through which they could push.

How hopeful the wind was in finding the wide channel of my stepfather. Through him it would find flesh against flesh, pursuing its eternal goal to right the first wronged flesh of a thousand years ago.

Tom was creative. I never realized what an artistic eye he had. He could find a new purpose for his hand at so many occasions. I have a loss of memory when I try to conjure up his creative eye from the past. He must have seen so many things with his artistic vision. How holding the fork incorrectly opened the door to release the generational pressure of his militaristic Virginia grandfather who brought him up extolling the virtues of dutifully returning the pain of life as parental care.

So much parental care Rick and I had. Our cousin visited and found himself helpless and subject to the return of the wind.

My brother and I looked at each other and almost smiled as a kind of pact silently formed between us. In that moment we agreed with our eyes that we were better than our cousin who had his hands covering his face because it hurt so much. The snuffles were all that was permitted because he had been properly told to stop crying... or else he would require some more parental care.

Rick and I did not feel so bad. We had been properly taught now. We looked at our cousin and thought... what a cry baby.

Forgiveness

I forgive myself for all I have done.
I forgive myself for all I have not done.
Goodbye.

The weight of my life is lying on the ground,
dissolving in the rain.

Spring Flood

How does someone leave your life?
They never leave.

There are so many trails emblazoned in your heart
that cannot be covered over.

Every time the water floods, it runs down the same trails
and little birds flutter up to branches.

Shiny fish wiggle into rivers,
and the whole jungle comes to drink and bathe rejoicing in the
spring flood.

It is the memory of you that awakens the spring in my being,
and being warm,
every emotion and dream come out of their hibernation,
and stretch and yawn and roll on the warm ground.

Beautiful, like the budding trees along the banks of the river,
colors find their way into every flower, frog, and bird,
and blood stirs and runs warm, and then hot,
until the day lights up,
and every creature sings, cackles, and roars.

Amidst the bright celebration,
distant thunder sounds, softly warning,
and all life is called back home,
away from a memory that had escaped,
and flowered with its dream of spring.

The animals pause, lifting their heads from the water,
and dissolve into the brown earth, hills, and sky.

The rivers dry up, and the birds flutter back down,
The yellow sun cools and rolls off into the distance,
and the dream of the warm day closes its eyes,
as evening wraps it soft cover of darkness over the world.

The old tree of my heart, reaches out into the night sky,
and little animals, wait on my branches,
like soft strokes of hope.

We are waiting for the light, for the heat of spring,
it's beautiful flood, burning with song and color.

How does someone leave your life?
They never leave.
The flood of their spring upon your earth
has marked you forever.

Last Light

Before night washes to mornings shore,
a shooting star crosses the silent boundary.

Its slash of memory,
calling all to return home.

Upon Earth

Behind the door.
The constellations.
You put on the apron of the universe,
and spread stars and life across the fields of earth.

An ancient wooden closet.
A holy cloth.
You put it on,
and sweep across the open fields,
watering the life of the world.

Within stone walls, your armor.
Walking down the stairs into earth,
you battle through the will of men in the world.

By the waters of the eternal lake,
you hold a soft cloth in your hand,
wiping the tears from a child's face,
asking the sky, "Why have you done this?"

Above the mountains, where only Gods can answer.
They consider the question, and speak,
"We have given you sun and seeds,
you have done what you wished."

A weathered farm shed stands in the field,
it's surface worn with surrender.
You lean the tired rake against the wall.

All your work is done.
You stand alone in the sun.
A seed has grown through the soil, green, shining.
You kneel down on the warm ground,
and kiss the brown earth.

Blade of grass

Brush of hot yellow sun grazes, strokes,
and paints the ripe green shine onto the full blade
thick and pungent, as if filled with grass blood,
seeping out damp life, unable to hold within the
thin edge of its gentle sweep.

And you my darling Angel, the same hot yellow brush
of sun caressing the beautiful brown loveliness of your face,
shining back like the answer and beginning of life infinite.
Radiant warmth melting, your gaze an embrace arresting.

Wind pressing the innocent fullness
just newly born this blade of gentle life at my feet.
Like so, your hair swirling, catching up your smile,
reaching the corner of your beautiful eye
opening deep and within.

In rapturous wonder, caught alive,
barely tasting the dream of you,
arching between life and reach,
its subtle glance like blows against my open surrender.

Seeing

I opened the cover of our skin
and looked out to the mountains,
but they were no longer there.

I saw a wall that had no colors or trees or animals
and people moved about inside.

I am kneeling in prayer,
and lifting my head,
see my brother,
but I do not know him.

He is covered.
Only his hands and face are not covered.
Is he afraid that the sun or the wind would touch his skin?

He speaks to the wind and is lost.
He cannot hear me as I put my arm around him.
He cannot feel me as I gesture for us to sit together.

In the distance there is a stampede of spirits I do not know.

My canoe is troubled.
We are alone on this river.
But now I know that will end.

My wife looks at me.
I see her.
And I know this way of seeing will end.

What Remains

I used to see you standing,
like a flower in the field,
breathing like wings opening,
and walk into your kitchen where life and rivers ran.

There in the hearth, your sun.

The shapes of us across the table,
until spirit only remained,
touched near a kind of light,
birthing what thought or words could not grasp.

You stood on the front porch waving goodbye.

You are no longer past the hinges on the swinging door.
I could call your name, and the towels where you pressed
your wet hands, would not answer.

Your river is flowing inside, spreading across the plains.

Under the Sun

Exploding run shot from dry earth,
great sudden leap,
crashing into prey,

sharp mouth,
neck breaking,
grapple and fall wrenching towards earth.

The roar of timeless death sounds,
and the great mother of the plain,
covers up her children again,

with silence and warm wind,
and all go back to drink by the water,
and sleep settles over quiet afternoon.

Calling

I saw the way home yesterday.
It was painted on the side of a building.
The message was clear.
You may leave this life and come home.

I was so comforted.
I didn't realize it could be that simple.
I thought I had to prove that I was real first,
that I was good in everyone's eyes.

I thought I had to stay here for all of you.
My wife my daughter, my employer,
my friends...

I looked at the side of the building again,
it was a little more faded now,
but I could still make it out.
You may come home.

I looked around in the traffic.
Life was so busy!

A thousand people living in such color and heat,
cars, trucks, others on bicycles, on motorcycles.
Throngs of people everywhere,
some with canes, some in wheel chairs,
and one begging for food to live.

They would not even know I was gone,
all these, all this life swirling in the sun of day.
They do not even know I'm alive,
they are all running, away from one moment,
and into the next.

I am trying to go home to the old house on the lake.
I am hoping to get there because I am tired
and falling asleep in the car.

But that is not it,
that is not why I am looking at the side of this building.

The light has turned green.
The traffic is moving slowly because life is clogged so full,
it is about to explode.

But it doesn't.
Everyone remains in their form,
their hands on their personal bags,
their hands pushing carts,
their hands on steering wheels,
their hands on their head,
because they are reliving the trauma of their life.
Their hands on a pack of cigarettes, holding hot dogs,
and cell phones, as if they have forgotten…

They are the pulse of the universe.
Do they even know?

The traffic is still slow. Good. I cannot believe that sign
on the side of the building was written for me so long ago.
I cannot believe it is still there, even more faded this third
time I am looking at it.

Come home.

Into the Dark

The feathers spoke,
do not go near,

but knowing once this chance only,
the touch of star and black sky clear,

my wings outstretched, through fiery strands,
past death shaking, its final warning.

Ansonia Lodge

I am in the heart of this old house.
Through the large beautiful windows I can see the
lake, especially now since the trees have lost their
leaves.

The wind threads around the house,
and lays not only trees bare of their last leaves,

but also lays the core of our hearts bare,
peeling back our past,
until glistening in surrender,
our morning stars are revealed and return like spring
leaves,

breathing into the face and fingers of dream,
to lay the paint of memory on canvas,
to write notes into strings of violins,
and to rise upward like morning dew finding the sky.

The wind threads through our life swirling and
holding us as we move towards the last door,
and stepping into the black night,
fall like a shooting star,
our friction into the new atmosphere of death making
us glow brighter,

and we travel across the sky fading softly into our last
light, leaving the living to wonder,
was it simply their imagination?
Or did an arc of tears and laughter just swim across
the daydream of their busy life?

Every soul stops and looks up for a moment,
wondering, knowing the wind has passed like a dream
they can't quite remember.

But not knowing how to hold the drawbridge of their life open
for a ship they cannot see, they shake their head to clear it,
but it doesn't go away because it is not in their head,
but in their heart,

and finally they give up searching,
and look down again into newspapers,
stirring pots over stoves and changing diapers,
feeling somehow that they are not the same,
and neither is the world,

and the wind blows across the roof and howls in the window.

This old house holds the traces from lives past.
Because we have been blessed and cursed to be human,
bits and pieces of life and dream hold on,
with clawing fingernails to cliffs of warm red blood.

They are washed over in the inevitable waterfall,
and only their trinkets remain,
like quiet little yelps,
as if even in death, they are still calling, "Remember me…"

The house stands, like an old beach,
with all the washed up humanity clinging to its insides.

Hanging in the wide old hallways,
paintings from unknown artists of another time silently hope
for living eyes to look and bring them back to life.

Two dark brown wooden tables stand on artfully curved legs
like obedient mythological creatures waiting to be set free from
the spell of human mastery.

The trees from which they came once waved beautifully in the songs of the wind, and like breaking the spirit of a wild horse, were bent and shaped and locked into the form of a table, forced forever to hold their miraculous flat surface in open surrender.

For where in nature is there a flat surface?
Only the frozen lake in winter, but even then,
the season of spring melts the beautiful mirror of her sun,
letting everything she held fall away.

A floral cloth has been placed so two corners hang over the front and back of one of the tables, like a waterfall, and the other two corners lay relaxed like bathers in the sand, with arms open, blissfully baking in the hot sun.

A large old black and white photograph of a man and woman that were just married rests on the flowery cloth and leans against the wall. The couple is holding hands and looking out,
asking us to join them.

Above the married couple,
a shelf holds the contents of the past;

A drawing of a young woman's face with a hand written poem underneath, two ceramic cats, their necks touching in a pose of affection, a little vase with a smiling dolphin, and other vases painted with pictures of flowers, young aristocratic lovers, and leaves.

There is one small picture on this shelf that holds my attention more than anything else, as if it is glowing. It looks like an old tintype that has faded. She is sitting, a book in her hand, a white apron, a white bonnet, and a white covering above her shoulders.

She is a servant, reading, her other hand resting upon an old
spinning wheel. In the picture, a table, a candle, a jug, and a
cup and saucer. The woman is beautiful; her long dark
braids flow down from her white bonnet and lay across her
white apron. The glass covering the old picture is cracked.

The tarnished delicate gold frame is shaped like a butterfly,
as if the picture knows it does not belong in this time,
and is trying to fly back home.

That is my fear and wonder,
that the whole house is trying to find its way home.

This is Ansonia Lodge, and spirits roam the halls and hover
outside the grand old house, and warmly fill every room
with their presence. The wide stairway creaks as one
ascends.

A cast iron radiator as big as a table heats up the room until
it is like summer inside. In between two large windows,
a fireplace and mantel stand like a beautiful work of art.
There are two doors along both sides of the fireplace
and they are filled with little shelves.

The Landlord, a man of wisdom, asked me to guess what
the shelves were used for in the past. To store small pieces
of wood? To hold little pots or pans to heat things over the
fire?

"They were bread warmers," He laughed.

I can open the window and walk right onto the roof. I can
sit with my back to the outside wall of the house and watch
the morning sun.

When I am inside, the windows are so big and the trees are so close that I feel as if I am in a tree house surrounded by graceful branches in the winter and a blanket of leaves in the summer.

The long driveway takes one away from the world. The land slopes down to the lake where a dock waits with a rowboat and a canoe to transport one into the water of peace and dream.

Cross-legged, sitting on the bed, facing the memories of bread warmers, a fireplace, and a hearty strong radiator keeping me warm against the cool blue of approaching winter, I cannot help but write as the silent voices swim and speak in the curves of the house and the wind blowing outside.

Another world flows through as the spirits of Ansonia Lodge share their lives. They pass through like a piano chord resonating, leaving its signature in the silence. The shape and color of how they feel is calm and soft. They are all here.

Crows caw and seagulls sing their painful cries as if they are messengers of the sad balance of the world. Geese honk their urgent call from afar, and small birds chirp and all are drawn to the lake, making soft feathers of music sweeping through the windows and shutters painted open.

And at last, the spirits change shifts in the widow's watch and wait.

We look at one another as I pass through its halls,
for we both share the same secret.

We have told no one, how we broke into pieces,
how we never fit into this world.
And now we are old.

I will fix your broken shutters. I will mend the shingles
on your roof. I will heal the scarred paint,
and smooth new coats all over you.

I will bow my head, and thank you for keeping me warm.
I look out the wide open window to the lake,
and wait for spring, with you, my friend,

and every picture hanging in your hall looks out from the
past, with the same hope and dream. I sleep and have a
strange dream where flowers are blooming through shining
ice in brilliant sun.

I wake, still old, still warm in this old house,
And finally know, that every moment is spring.

Returning

Passing through air to earth,
rustling the leaves of the forest,
unfolding upon shoulders sleep it's gentle touch.

Traces and outlines of skin and time,
float down like invisible feathers,
from wings of parents who have left,
the brush of life sparkling in every pore of your skin.

The tapestry of the universe covers your shoulders,
it's thread woven from a thousand dreams.

Inscribing every cornerstone,
mapping messages on the bark of trees
and upon the water.

Here

"Are you still here?" we ask.
Some of us say we feel you and some of us aren't sure.

We stand by the trees, the beach, or in the backyard.
Sometimes we ask for you to visit in our dreams.

We're looking to talk with you.
We can no longer call on the phone or drop by to visit.
We can only commune through our faith.

Sometimes things happen, like when I talked to you while
looking into the night sky and a beautiful shooting star
appeared.

One of your dear friends told me their TV turned on by itself
and was full of static. Your husband said that he talks with you
at the end of the day, because that is when you used to call him
when you were traveling, to let him know you were okay.

I was hoping you would make a physical appearance, like
materializing in front of me and having a conversation. Some
of our mutual friends have said they have talked to you but
haven't heard anything back. I don't know if they are not being
sensitive enough, or if you no longer exist in any realm, and they
are just being honest.

You chose cremation, so none of us can speak with you at your
grave. Your ashes were scattered by your tree where you used
to talk with the universe. I guess we could make a pilgrimage to
your back yard and talk to you near your tree.

But knowing you, I think you would say we should talk with you
from wherever we are.

When I talk with you, I make a point of stopping and listening to the silence. That's when I sense your presence. Sometimes, a thought occurs to me in the moment of speaking with you, as if you can't wait to tell me something.

I've noticed how your presence feels different now as compared to immediately after you passed away.
It felt like you were closer right after you left us, like you were in the air in the room. Now you are farther away and I have to talk with you for a while before you come back.

Sometimes I think I should not talk to you because you are busy where you are and you'd want me to move on with my life.

Your leaving is a lesson to us.
Who are we now without you?
When you were here, everything was magical.

Now, with you gone, I'm falling back into my old habits, and part of me doesn't want to bother with anything, as if there's no point, because you're not here to share it.

But sometimes, when I least expect it, I will feel a moment of union. I'll see the morning sun coming into the room, and without really thinking about it, I'll begin talking with you as if you had never left.

I'll say "The sun is so beautiful coming through the window," and somehow I'll know you are there.
Or I'll be driving and will just ask, "How are you?" and I'll feel a quiet knowing.

You left a big hole in our lives.
At first it was so empty all we could do was cry,
but that emptiness allowed our rivers to return.

You came like a flower in the farmer's field, and as your
petals blew away, the seeds of our time began to open.

In an odd way, it feels like we have expanded inside.
Like there's more room for everything.

More room to hold everyone in our arms,
like when you held us in yours.

I used to keep to myself because I was not wanted, but you
made me feel like I was the dream blessing the world.

That was your gift to all of us. You let us know that there
was nothing wrong with us, that in fact, we were wonderful.

So if I say, "Hey, how's it going up there?"
Forgive me. I love you.

Promise

You cannot keep the colors of autumn.
Autumn comes and goes.

There is no claim on this moment,
however sweet and beautiful it may be.

You must move on,
and allow the cold white winter to take its place,
and the trickling warmth of spring as it creeps in,
quietly kind and forgiving.

Neither memory, nor hopeful dream,
they too like leaves fall and blow away.

Like children running after,
we hope to catch something,
that we don't know is already gone.

And how we celebrate each leaf caught
before touching the ground,
as if we halted the fate of the world,
and held it safe in our hand.

But colorful and graceful as its flight may have been,
it is not long before you must let go.

Even if you store it away in a book,
and years later, remember a gentle tumble from the sky,
and maybe even, the state of your heart.

Home

In your eyes I used to see,

Stars

Sun

Moon…

A lake

Quiet, still…

I would look, and become lost within,
and you would look back, open as the wind.

Perhaps another life will let me find you again.

Distant

It was time for you to go.

We could not follow,
as you flew through the straw of sunlit fields,
your windy light weaving.

We remained.
Our wings folded,
and fell into the parting sea.

Days

We will pass...
and all that we have known.

We will look upon the earth
and see a softly lit planet in the sun as one moment,
like a drop of rain born in the sky.

Like when you told your child
how little crumbs fall on the floor,
and to try to eat over the plate,

and when you pressed the gas pedal a little harder,
and the car jumped forward,
and calling out, "Remember to close the front door,"

and your husband smiling at the door,
a moment when everything was right,
and how he looked like a boy when you first met.

What do those little flits of memory mean,
against the silent pull and turn of earth?

I will touch you, as waving straw colored grass,
as a mother holds her child's hand,
stepping over the rock in the field.

As a wave swirls around your feet on the sandy beach.
Holding the one birthday candle to light the others.

I loved my child,
the wind blew.

Opening

Between the early morning of gentle hope,
and the soft evening of story books closing,

we sail into the wind,
dressed in the light of burning suns,
playing in the waves of time
as they lap against our shore.

Lightning wakes us from sleep,
and our petals open,
as if we really were a flower after all.

It is a soft morning,
and we rise from the floor of the forest,
running into fields of sun,
and stretch our neck to leaves and stars,
until they fill our bellies and we lay down full,
dreaming under the quiet blanket of night.

Wind blows against our new skin and wings,
we don't know why we are walking,
with feet and beautiful eyes through a dream,
past trees, and animals bounding over tall grass.

Ah...

I am merely a balance
a scale
a point in the center

A point of balance
seeking equal weight
within the burning sun

Fear and Scar

The fear and scars of my past stay close like friends.
They walk with me now, their old swords sharp and ready.

I used to call them all the time.
But now we're getting older and can't be bothered to fight
about every little thing. Maybe that's it, you live long enough,
and realize, all you ever wanted was the warm light of
morning.

We look at the sunrise together.
"Do you need us now?" they ask.

In the silence, the sunrise glows like golden hope.

Fear and Scar look at me, and I realize, they will die soon.

In the morning glow, I take their hands.

"I have needed you my whole life, my dear Fear and Scar,
but to look at a sunrise?"

We walk to the water, stepping into the creaking rickety boat
with its old wooden oars.

Fear and Scar ask again if they should press themselves close,
because the boat might sink and the water is cold.

They are wearing warm thick coats as if they are afraid of
something.

"You guys, come here." I say. They are a bit tentative in the
front of the boat, as if they are afraid I will take something
from them.

I will.

I give them big hug, and their sharp edges disappear...

...they feel the warm heat of my embrace
and start changing into a plant and a lamb.
They look at themselves and wonder what happened.

In the distance, there is a roar from high above.
Something is cutting open the sky.

The Father of Fear and Scar,
a great dead gray tiger in the wind.

I forget the warmth our embrace and allow the kite of my fear
to reel wildly out of my chest, pulling raw scars out naked,
burning like birds from fire in the forest.

The dead gray tiger rears up,
and the dread of the world descends.

The day wrenches forward with its heavy pressing
and leans in hard, crushing every hope in tangles of strewn
ropes and steel claws ripping, tying hearts to wooden boards,
and prying them bare, as if nothing ever done trailed without
its scars.

Plant and lamb look at me, fearful that they will be eaten for
allowing themselves to change.

We spill into each other's arms shaking in the little boat,
and freeze like rabbits in the field.

But the sharp claws hold themselves back for a moment.

The dead gray tiger has just smelled fresh coffee brewing
somewhere in the universe and decides to turn around
and have a cup.

I hope there is enough cream and sugar for him.
A peaceful silence returns.
Our eyes open and we wonder if he was ever there at all?
Or if we just imagine the most horrible things.

But looking up, there is a rip in the sky where he had torn it
shred to shred.

Soft yellow light is coming through...the rip heals,
and the warm touch of morning sun
reminds us that we are safe.

The dead gray tiger may come back,
but for now, there is too much fragrance in the wind,
it will not allow any door to open that is not sweet.

The balance of this day tilts its soft head
towards beautiful things grown from soft soil and reflections
in hopeful eyes.

They look at me with a funny expression on their faces.
 "What happened to us? Who are we now?" They ask.

"You are my Fear and my Scar,"
I remind them both with a smile.

They look at each other feeling embarrassed.
The coats look so silly on them.

I help them out of their coats
and lay them down on the bottom of the boat.

We are near the middle of the lake now.

They seem exhausted from their transformation
and the threat of the dead gray tiger in the sky.
They are having trouble staying awake.
"Go to sleep, my Fear."

The lamb curls itself into the coats on the bottom of the boat
and closes its eyes into the most peaceful sleep it has ever known.

I ask my Scar to close it's eyes and rest.
The plant unfurls every stem and leaf,
revealing the deepest glossy green shine I have ever seen.
It releases its stiff posture and begins to sway
in the light touch of the wind.

I row the old rickety boat,
gently pulling the oars in and out of the water, and rest.

We glide silently,
as silently and quietly as is possible on earth,
the sun's touch on my shoulders like honey pouring through.

I curl into the bottom of the boat.
The lamb shifts in its sleep to make space for me,
the plant lays itself across us both,
and the little boat moves like a star
in the center of the universe.

Window

Near the end of our days, our loved ones come to visit.
We are in bed.

We can see the eyes and the head staring at us close,
surrounding us with presence, like water rushing into
a sinking submarine, presence spills into every opening
of our ears and eyes, and finally, reaches our heart,
and emotions flow like tidal waves.

We apologize as tears spill out of our face,
and the face looking down at us holds our hand,
and fills up with ocean, and spills over, and words
stumble out, unsure of their way, staggering.

They say things like, "It's ok," and their hands rest on
our chest, as if to keep our heart from leaving.

Doors within doors open, and we are floating near the
top of the room, looking down. We see our body and
the person leaning over our bed, our brother, our friend,
come to visit.

They gently call our name, and we know we are not
there.

Sailing Birth

A last breath swirls up to stars and sun,
and circling around earth returns,
as fiery spark cracking into life sharply born.

Forgiveness remembers the sand of her shore,
and softly laps against your feet.

Traces stream from the fire of your day,
like signals across the distant mountain.

Budding into leaves and Cottonwood,
the river swirls through your blood,
and rises into the sky.

You are the light upon straw in the field,
and the wings above the earth.

Transparent

Their dreams fall into the world,
chanting softly through the old chair,
singing through wolf hide.

Cracking split into hard wood,
laying bare the heart of the old tree's open pasture.

Their spears thrown into the future,
flying over continents and centuries,

coming to rest in the paper on the desk,
and the wooden vase on the shelf.

It is here.
In the room.

Speaking through the language of their form,
waiting like humble servants,

created by their masters a thousand years ago,
waiting for us to touch them again.

The You in Me

I close my eyes and think of you.
Your body and shape are part of it.
But it is more your face,
and even more than that,
it is your eyes.

They are slightly crooked, did you know that?
I have kept that secret lovely aspect of you quietly in my heart.

But the you that resides in me is more than any physical aspect.
It is the essence of your being making its home in my heart.

I just feel who you are. Inside me. Almost all the time.

That's it.

I could hug myself knowing you are in there too.
But it is too much me, and not enough you.

It is only when we are in the same space,
That the You In Me and the you standing right there,
become one.

Then the world begins to glow, and I know I am home.

But now, I wait for you, and the You In Me looks at me with
questioning eyes asking,

"Is she coming?"

I answer "No," and the You In Me says… "Oh..." and waits.

A few days later the You In Me will ask again.
And usually it is the same answer.

"No, she is not coming."

The You In Me decides it doesn't want to wait any longer,
it is ready to join the rest of itself,
the you that is outside of me.

It tries to rejoin itself through letters and prayers and even dreams.

Every night the world becomes still.
So still that the beat of my heart seems loud.
I can feel the blood rushing through my veins.

Then the You In Me will ask in its most innocent way,
"When can I find the rest of me?"

"I don't know." I answer.
And the You In Me begins to cry.

"There there now, it will be okay," I say quietly, and brush
the tears from its eyes, and the You In Me looks up like the
sorrow of the world.

The You In Me still aches. It looks out the window every day
hoping to see the loving mother of itself.

"Where are you dear dear mother of myself?"

Sometimes, it begins to forget who it is.
I am suddenly afraid. Who will I be without the You In Me?
Will I disappear too?

We walk in the open fields.

"Oh, look at how beautiful everything is," we say to each other.

The You In Me runs off and disappears into the woods.

I lay on the tall grass and the long day stretches out warm and still.

I close my eyes and disappear into dream.
I am walking hand in hand with the mother of the You In Me. We embrace and become the sun.

A light brush touches my face, I open my eyes and see only blue sky and the tops of feathery grass waving.

I stand, alone, free, and head for home.

But running out from the woods like a child that can't wait to tell you what she just discovered, the You In Me comes bounding towards me like a playful doe.

I kneel down and sigh. The You In Me jumps into my arms and calls my name, and reminds me that she will be with me forever.

Sun

I opened my heart like a door,
I opened my heart like a river,
I opened my heart like the rain.

You poured in like a waterfall,
You poured in like all the birds migrating home,
You poured in like every flower opening.

Tall Tree

Deep within the forest, paws, wings, and hooves gathered.

Tall Tree looked down at the little animals circled around his roots and held out his branches.

He cleared his throat and shook his leaves. A few of his children floated down and settled on the ground.

"I would like to tell you about Walking Leaf."

The animals drew in a little closer. Tall Tree continued.

"She is the wind and blood inside us.
She is the water of the lake,
and the heat of the sun.
She comes in the form of a woman,
embracing the world through the touch of her heart."

Tall Tree paused and Squirrel asked, "What does she look like?"

"She is brown like the earth,
her hair is black and grey like a waterfall across her shoulders.
Her eyes are made from the sun in spring,
and to look at her is to return home."

"But many are like that," Squirrel continued.
"How will I know it is her?"

Tall Tree smiled to himself, knowing that none in the forest were as Walking Leaf.

"Do you know your mother?" Tall Tree asked.

"Of course, I would know my mom anywhere." Squirrel Said.

"Would you know her from all the other mothers in the forest?"

"Of course I would know her from all the mothers in the forest!" Squirrel exclaimed, suddenly proud.

"So it is, that you will know Walking Leaf," Tall Tree said quietly.

"But my mom gave birth to me, she brought me into the forest and taught me how to gather nuts, and how to dig, and where to hide them. She taught me everything. I know my mom." And then Squirrel looked to the ground and cried.

Baby Deer looked at the ground and sniffled too, because she no longer had a mother.
And that is why she loved to jump as high as she could, because she could feel her mother jumping with her.

"Walking Leaf gave birth to all of us," Tall Tree said softly.

Squirrel looked like he wasn't ready to hear anymore.
He didn't know why a tear had fallen out of his eye.

It was like a little fish was swimming inside trying to find its way home, but it couldn't, so it bumped into the window of Squirrel's eye, and a little of the sea spilled out into the world of the forest.

"That is why tears are magic," Tall Tree said

"What?" Squirrel looked up, and wondered how Tall Tree could know.

He glanced at Baby Deer who was sniffling into the ground, and she closed her eyes and looked away.

"When you see Walking Leaf, Squirrel, she will look upon you and you will know you are the sun and the wind."

"But I don't want to be the sun and the wind," Squirrel said,
and ran into the curve of Tall Tree's branch and cried.
A few leaves saw their own sorrow and floated down to
make a blanket for Squirrel who went to sleep and dreamed.
Baby Deer looked up and realized she couldn't climb Tall Tree
to comfort Squirrel, and looked over to Sparrow and Raccoon.

A softness poured out between them and they turned to
Tall Tree.

"I have heard from Heart of My Branch,
in the land near the water...he has felt the embrace of
Walking Leaf, because she is weak and leans against him,
so she will not fall to earth."

"Heart of My Branch has called for the healing wind."

Raccoon stood up, "I am so sorry to ask, Tall Tree,
because I see this is very deep within your trunk,
but please forgive me, is not Walking Leaf a legend,
a simple story of the forest?"

Tall Tree smiled kindly and said, "Nothing is ever known
Raccoon, only cries in the wind and cries in the heart."

"Does Walking Leaf cry?" Raccoon asked.

"Walking Leaf cries, and Heart of My Branch cries,
and the ground of earth cries, until my roots tremble,
and I see into the land of Heart of My Branch."

"Do you see into the land because you are so tall?"

"No, I am not tall enough to see into the land of
Heart of My Branch."

"Do you see because your leaves return full with stories
and news?"

"My leaves never return, I am always saying goodbye forever."

"Did you say you saw a picture as your roots trembled?"
Raccoon asked.

"Yes, and it was clear as the ring and shine of the water bell."

And all the animals were still because they heard the water bell in the morning, but did not know why it should ring into this world.

Raccoon had never thought to venture very deep into his heart, but found himself suddenly caught in a current of wonder.
He was not sure whether he could even ask, but it burst out of his mouth before he could stop himself.

"Can you show me the picture?"

Raccoon was unsure whether Tall Tree would look sternly or gently upon him.

"I will give it to all of you," Tall Tree answered.

Raccoon sensed a deep stirring,
as if something was about to happen.
Sparrow, who had been flitting his little head from side to side, stopped flitting.

Baby Deer tilted her head up, and Squirrel, who had been sleeping, opened one eye and listened.

Tall Tree spoke: "Let us listen together."

Squirrel stirred and shook off his blanket of leaves and ran down Tall Tree's wide trunk to the ground.
The little animals folded their legs under their soft bellies, and leaned their heads until their ears touched the ground.
They looked like soft fluffy dreams abandoned to the bliss of the earth.

Just then the sun came out from behind the clouds
and spilled like warm glowing feathers.

The animals opened their soul windows
and the little rivers inside their ticking hearts stopped running.

There was Heart of My Branch and Running Stream.

The little animals shivered for a moment, returning to the home
they had forgotten.

This was so familiar…from dreams…and reflections in the water.

And what was that near Heart of My Branch?
It was a little fuzzy,
but then Squirrel, Raccoon, Sparrow, and Baby Deer
felt it again like the ring and shine of the water bell.

Another heart!

Was Heart of My Branch two trees they wondered?
And as they wondered,
they felt the guiding low whoosh of Tall Tree touch the soil
to open the tunnel between all things a little wider.

And there was Walking Leaf, her heart beating so close to
Heart of My Branch.

And in the same moment the animals realized that Walking
Leaf was real, they also realized that she leaned because she
was weak, and Heart of My Branch leaned, trying to hold
Walking Leaf up.

The picture of Walking Leaf and Heart of My Branch
and Running Stream swam through the soil to every creature.

"What shall we do?" asked Sparrow.

Baby Deer sniffled a little and wiped her nose on the grass.

Tall Tree took in a deep breath.

"I will call the healing wind."

"I will give her my feathers," tweeted Sparrow.

"I will give her my acorns," said Squirrel.

"I will go to her and keep her warm," said Baby Deer.

And Raccoon said, "I will guard her home."

And Tall Tree's sap ran.

Lost

I am reaching for what is under your skin,
running in your blood.

I am reaching for a shape,
the position of bones under a face.

Opening the door of another being,
I look in the closet for the life I misplaced.

You

Like a dog shaking the wet from its coat,
I quiver as you turn inside.

Like wearing another person,
weighted with wonder and charms.

The sea of your shore,
swims in my blood and everything I touch.

Your hand, my hand, the same flesh,
your words, my words, the same mouth, your heart, my heart,
soaked in the red thrashing pulse of rivers red rapids twisting.

I turn, and your presence slams like a great wave against the
ship of my being. I am sharped and shocked onto the path
of your dream.

Like walking from cloud to cloud above where birds can fly,
I follow the impressions in the deep snow,

There, almost visible, a whisper.

The long arm of your summer pulls me out from sleep,
towards the floating stars and shiny mud softly thick and cool
between laughter's wings all burble and wiggle warm.

And waking, always waking.
I hear you, in the drop of rain and hail and crackly dry leaves
windy brushing blow, your name, soft and pulling.

Returning to the circle of things born,
My arms reach out, like a ballerina and a beggar.

Tears of the Warm Day

You are in this spring day,
moving like a hidden charm across the land,
speaking through dreams in the wind.

Your spirit leaves so many question marks hovering,
like bees unable to find their flowers.

We follow your scent,
but wash upon an empty shore.

You had picked out a life
that was the most beautiful shell on the beach,
and threw it into the sky,
like flowers behind the bride.

Bird in the Field

Little Bird, you are not moving,
standing in the shadow of sun's last arm of light.

You do not step or flutter a wing as we come close,
silent with unuttered words of caution,
holding the air fixed like a forbidden gate between us.

It is a language between man and bird,
to not come any closer,
into this sacred space,
as wide as the world, and private as the deepest cave.

Solemnly standing,
unable to move,
bathed in sacred stillness,
the holy space of your parting.

On one leg,
alone in the field,
nesting into the sphere of another world,
burning an invisible ring around your little feathered heart.

We are sorry to have tread near,
we thought only to find the sky,
and dreams hiding in the field,
and stumbled instead, upon a little feather breathing.

I cannot look away from you in the vacuum of this space,
opening a tunnel into the sky.

We are without speech, and shamed, that we did not know,
that a little bit of feather and breath, and a staring eye
older than the world, would freeze us into statues.

Rust

You are a young river, dancing from shore to shore.
I am a painting, hanging on a wall.

You are a bird having just touched the water.
I am a weathered statue, still in the sun.

You are a song, sung from laughing children.
I am old bones in a museum.

You are a game of tag, "Gotcha! You're it!"
I am the broken fence you have trampled over.

You are pedaling as fast as you can,
I am the training wheels in the corner of the garage.

You are curious eyes lighting up with wonder,
I am the lonely house falling apart in the field.

You are the kiss of first love,
I am the old letter in the desk.

Sorrow's Seed

Every morning,
In the space open for spirits,
I wait.

But it does not come,
and sadness draws out,
feeling this space,
so empty and still.

Your absence weighs quietly.

But I must breathe,
and somehow open my eyes,
and look upon the day.

Without warning,
the rapids of a wild untamed river,
surge up into my chest,
twisting and churning,

and before I can ask the river to stop,
It overflows its banks,
and floods the valleys,
and even the mountains are covered.

Like Noah, floating upon the silent water,
safe within the fragile ark of life,
a speck on the wide ocean.

Softly, sounds rise from the deck below.
Innocent animals neigh and bark and flutter and sing
and rock back and forth within the arms of the great sea
of faith and dreams.

Echoes of land swim,
with memories of hands touching,
and feet on warm earth.

The ark groans,
its timbers creaking,

lit like a jewel within the warm sun of day,
remembering every breath and sparrow.

But sorrow does not last forever,
looking into the sun,
her hands rise in supplication,
and she dissolves in the wind.

Exhausted, the great flood recedes,
weary, and lies down,

back into its valleys and streams,
within the familiar embrace of the arms of the world.
The sun lays itself on land,
warming into green leaves and red blood.

Wondrous creatures return,
craning their necks to drink,
from lakes and rivers,
sweet and cool in the honeysuckle scent of day.

As they sleep in afternoon sun,
the pendulum of sky swings away from sorrow's great flood,
into her barren plain.

The arm of the desert's dry sword
slashes across the ocean and slays the running waves,
and the banks of the rivers lay flat,
unable to hold their promise.

The mouth of the desert exhales its dry breath,
upon which no arc can sail,
and hooves, hands, and eyes wait beneath the great scale,
as mercy finds the balance of her sway.

The blanket of night rolls over all creation,
turning their eyes into dream,
as they hover over the chasm of uncertainty and promise,

and emerging,
from communion with the stars,
morning opens...

A wayward floating seed,
bumps and brushes,
along the dusty earth,

and drifts upward, guided in the hands of the wind,
that it should not die on dry ground,

sweeping along unseen paths of air,
like silent horses,
riding into the waiting sky.

Meadows, trees, and fields below,
lay themselves open as soft story pages of quilted patchwork,
written, knitted, and painted with breath.

Creatures that run lay down in the fields,
along with the bending grass and wait at the door of their end,
for the will of the sky to change.

The moon and sun shepherd
the traveling seed along its journey,
higher than the tallest tree,
close to the night stars near the edge of the world.

Morning paints itself onto earth once more,
and the little seed passes through the last door of the sky.
From beyond time, the ancient will of life stirs.

The bell of a thousand years rings,
and the sounds of wind and rain come rushing in,
as if the door of the universe had been left open.

Silent lightning flashes across the sky,
transparent edges begin to form,
and the weeping seed falls to earth...

Down past the parched bird circling in the hot dry air,
Down past the burned leaf floating like an omen in the wind.
Down past the tops of the weeping mountains,
having lost the cover of their white snows,

Down past the tops of the trees in the lowlands,
their spring buds drooping like sad bells
having forgotten to ring.

And into... the open unfurled hand of nature.
She, having let go of life's last little scurry,
lay without raiment, pure, in giving pose.
Waters touch upon her hand, enough.

Red blood and green leaves return to her face.
Earth stirs from its dry sleep,
and a shooting star streaks across the sky,
a seed of the universe, holding the memory of the world.

Slowly, on unsteady legs, a newborn colt tries to stand,
and wobbly, moves forward,
jumping and kicking like little sparks.

And far above, beyond where eye can see,
another dream is born, and one more drop of water falls.

It is too dry to hope,
but hope cannot hold herself back,
even though she is lying twisted and mangled,
she can still remember her name,
and reaches to touch the sky.

Two drops have fallen,
and two dreams swim into the world.

Earth, standing before the spirit of its own light, delivers itself.
The universe nods, its balance restored,
and turns its eye to the multitude of stars and life,
tending its garden of infinity.

Rain falls and water flows into the valley, like petals of spring.
Every grain wakes into its sparkling birth.

Thankful cries pour into the world,
and darkened eyes open.
You are laughing.
We are all laughing under sun and wind,
ringing the balance of the scale.

Turning from the heavy work in your hand,
you look up,

and warmth springs from a well so full,
that we glow with radiance.

I wake from the sleep of sorrow's hand,
and feel the sun's comforting arm across my chest.
Unbounded, a deep, slow river flows.

Standing before the spirit of my own light,
when all things are near their end.

Your Voice

The sound of your voice,
is why there are leaves
and candles in still places
and water like a mirror of heaven.

Dear,

I never knew they could stretch you out to fill the whole world.
But there you are, across heaven and earth,
laid over the soft green brush of the forest, and the lapping
blue of sea.

There you are, in the space in the center of my room,
like a warmth of radiant silence holding its place,
like a marker of the soul of the world.

I am lifted up and out of the window, into your arms.

You are so big like a giant but not so scary,
and then we are the same again,
talking like we always did,
reaching into each others hearts like ladling out soup,
until we are full and warm, in a blanket of stars.

It is not unusual then, to hover over our homes and our town,
and to visit everyone in church and temple, and on their knees
at home, trying to join us, and then they do,

galloping up to us like horses,
cresting into wings,
and sailing down into the hands of children,
like kites and balsa wood gliders on the wind.

We laugh and cry until our rain fills the fruit of giving branches,
like gentle hearts dreamed from earth.

Walking softly into tomorrow and singing into dream, we waft
in and out of night and day and birth and death, like a stream
of river's memory, and every hand reaches towards the soft
light of your passing, like little seeds, looking for their home.

Memoir: Leaving

They took me to the airport.
I don't remember packing and considering what to bring.
I don't remember the clothes I put in the suitcase.
I don't remember the suitcase. I don't remember saying goodbye
to my friends. I don't remember taking a moment with my dog.
I don't remember looking at my room, or the house, or the yard,
or the school or the park that lay beyond.
There was no goodbye to any of it.
I have a vague image of myself in a denim jacket.

My stepfather shook my hand and said good luck. He had a
smile that looked guilty and confused at the same time.

The firm press of his handshake seemed to suggest equality, as
if this was the first sign of my manhood that was strong enough
for him to respect. For a moment, our dislike of each other
was replaced by something we could both agree on. My leaving.
That was the only unity my stepfather and I shared together.
Becoming free of each other.

My mom hugged me and cried. She said things that were all
useless and I waited for her to be done.

My brother and I shook hands because we didn't know what
else to do. Under the surface of our skin we knew I was
abandoning him.

I turned to go. All the untended broken moments we would
never be able to fix, all the times we had meant to say, I love
you, but never did, and all the things we would never share
together. He suddenly realized that the hopes of all these
things were being ripped away from him forever.

His eyes widened and he seemed to go into shock and began
to cry. My mom held him and they wept in each others arms.
My stepfather stood there, out of time, and out of place,
not knowing what to do, or what he had done.

I couldn't wait to get away from the ugly unhappy lie
we had all been living.

It was a relief and a trauma for all of us.
I walked away, and turned back for one last look.
What if I never saw them again?
Emotion flitted somewhere in my chest,
but it was so deeply buried.

Was I making a terrible mistake?

I waved, and saw them waving back and thought…
goodbye…
and walked onto the plane.

Spirit Dream

How wonderful it is to swim through forests,
and to make them breathe again,
to wag tails, and open into buds and wildflowers.

Shall I raise you again?
It a long swim through hopes and dreams,
animating eyes and souls until breath moves forward
and hands touch and cities are built.

I have no choice I laugh to myself,

and up you go,
into parents hands,
holding the hope of life.

Huntress

Your fur was orange and so warm underneath that when I ran
near your skin, I knew this was where the heat of the world
came from, and sparks inside speckled out like yellow suns.

The sky was a different color then,
and your breath pulled from the center of the world,
its rumbling roar like the sound of distant thunder walking.

The weight of a thousand predatory years in the jungle,
considered the balance, as plains rushed below,

and your heavy paws opened another sun,
its red streams warm,

glistening into the heat of life, along the banks of the river,
your neck turning to the world.

The Tribe and the River

We ran from the fire in the forest.
We swam from the wreck at sea.
We left the burning desert.
We descended from the mountain.

"Where are you all going?" You asked.

"We are trying to survive." We answered.

"Here," You said, and handed us a book.

We opened it hoping we could be healed,
but there was nothing upon the pages.

We had hoped that we would become like God,
but we remained plain.

You returned our questioning gaze with silence.

"Who are you, who would give us a book of nothing?"

"It is all there," You said.

"Do you not understand our suffering? We are trying to eat
and live, of what use is this? Hand me a spear, show me where
the fruit grows, then you will be welcome within our tribe.
Or are you not of this world? Do you not need to eat, and drink
from the river?"

"I do not eat, or drink from the river."

"Well, You Who Does Not Eat Or Drink From The River,
leave us."

You did not move or run from us. We searched the book again, unsure if you were a God, and wondered if perhaps we were unable to discern the mystery of your hidden gift.

The gray sky opened into sun.
The plains breathed.

A shadow passed over the ground,
the wisdom of old feathers whispering their secret.

"Where is the story of the hunter, the field, the birth, the warrior, where is the hand upon the hut and the climbing tree?"

"It is for you to write," you said.

"Our life is already written in the stories of our ancestors, we have the living river full with fish and water to drink.

Our fathers have spoken under the stars of night,
of what a man can do between coming into the world
and returning to the sky."

Our spears rested on your flesh but you did not move.

"Leave us! Fool from the wind." we commanded, and watched the beginning of your blood reveal that you were merely one who walked.

"This will become the book of your life," you said.

"Do not mock us," We spoke. "Our lives are sacred whether written in a book or in the sky or the grass of the field.

"Let me drive this spirit away," One of us called out, and slashed a line across your chest.

"May I see the book?" You asked, ignoring the line upon your skin and the red life seeping away.

We withdrew a step and returned the book to you. It was heavy, of many pages.

We held the push of death close.

"What are you looking for?" you asked.

"Whether you are from the mud or from the sun I do not know, but I will tell you one more time, that you may understand and live, or die, it is your choice.

We are looking to be healed, we are looking for rain, we are looking for the bees and their honey, we are looking for the fish in the river, we are looking for days that will warm our children.

"It is in your blood," you said.

"I am sorry that you do not love the breath of your life, You Who Does Not Eat Or Drink From The River, what we are looking for is not in our blood. Your answer is not worthy of the animals and trees, who know their purpose."

Unaffected by the threat of our spears, you turned a few of the empty pages and looked into the sky.

Of what world you came from, or whether you walked on earth we did not know.

You closed the book, and spoke; "There once was a great rain, and though it was wished for, it washed away the world."

We thrust our spears into your heart.

You fell like one of us. How foolish that we believed for a moment, You Who Does Not Eat Or Drink From The River, that you might have been from the sky.

We threw you and the book-with-no-writing into the river. You swept quickly from us in the rushing water.

We thanked the forest for the return of things we understood, of animals and the moon.

Night came welcoming and familiar, reassuring our troubled day, that all things pass, even spirits from the unknown.

We might have dreamed of hunting the pig or finding the lake in the clouds but we did not. Another dream is come to us all.

You Who Does Not Eat Or Drink From The River are opening the book. It is full of words and stories.

The hunter, the field, the birth, the warrior, the hand upon the hut and the climbing tree. It is upon every page.

Offering

I know the thousand suns
that are the rivers of your blood.

I give of the ram and the goat,
until my prayer
reaches the wind of your heart.

The fire on the altar rises,
and the listening sky
washes the open field.

Weight

Tight against your finger, no longer sure,
if you are pulling the trigger,
or if it is pressing its knife edge into your skin.

The stains of dirt and blood have become invisible.
The color of the sky does not matter.

A scream...like a bar of solid metal fixed in eternity... cracks,
as the tripwire explodes into a concentration of entangled lines
of hot bullets, dense within the compressed weight of finality's
instant decision.

Is the library book overdue? Did I not return it in time?
How much does the fine of my life cost?
I did pay it, didn't I?

A deafening explosion freezes the world.
A drop of silence falls.

...did I pay it?

Renewed crackling trails of death wildly seek the heat of their
inertia, shredding plants, cloth, and tree bark into particles and
spray, and mother comes close to read a night story by the
wild springing ratchet of death. It is easy to walk here.

It is warm in my chest,
I am giving up one package after another,
they are all being kindly and thoughtfully gathered,
exchanging each one for the weight of my life.

I did not know, I had carried them for so long.
It is easy to let go now. What were your names?
Oh, you were my wife, and you were my daughter, and I smile.

Goodbye Again

I can feel you saying goodbye now.
Not the kind of goodbye like waving
your hand when you were here,
but the kind of goodbye from beyond this world.

I had gotten used to talking to you way over there.
At first, it was like talking to the trees or the water
or the stars. I used to hear you in all those places.
But now, you are talking to me from so far away,
I am not sure.

If I do not lie to myself,
I think you are saying goodbye again.
I sense you are writing a last letter
from your cottage beyond the stars.

***

Dear friend,
I walked as spirit between our worlds.
Now that path is gone.
I see you on earth trying to remember me.

Before the last part of me dissolves,
I want to say goodbye again, goodbye, because I knew you,
because we were joined together like the beginning of light.
Even from here, I can feel the traces of that.

I am disappearing, spreading into space.
I can no longer appear in your dreams
or speak through the water.

I was but a yellow flower in the sun.

The universe is holding me like my mother.
There is so much to learn. I want to become the stars.

Your pull holds me to earth and I cannot leave.
For days and weeks and months I have been visiting you,
your hand and mine clasped together,
as I help you onto the shore of your life.

I could become flesh again,
but it is time for you to feel the glory of the sun alone.

This is the last step.
This is my last lesson.
I am shedding who I am,

And then, I can hold you forever,
but I will not have my name or memory,
or a message, except to say,
live my dear, I am you now.

Born

A thousand years ago,
a wave washed upon this shore
filled with the breathing earth.

This great old tree stands.
A blade of grass waves in the wind.

Looking up from soil to find its rain,
a seed pushes out from soft ground,

glowing full with earth blood,
alive in the wind of amber sunset.

Guardian

I grew, and found myself split between two continents,
and four, and then I could no longer keep count.
I listened to the fish jumping from the water,
and heard the panting wolf run to catch its prey.

I lifted my branches and gave homes to the birds.

A little girl climbed up and called to her friends,
"Come on, it's easy," and they pulled themselves
up laughing in the leaves.

Of myself, I give my body,
for homes, chairs, shelves, walking canes, fruit, and leaves.
I ask only that you allow me to have what you wipe off the
bottom of your shoes.

Dirt...

And what you shield yourself from under your roof.

Rain...

I take what you do not want,
and make everything you need.
I do not run after you with accusations,
or attack you for what you have,
or cry that I do not have enough.

I sing when the wind rustles through my leaves
and brings your breath,
and hold myself quietly as a picture,
in a midsummer day.

I am trustworthy.
I will be outside your window for days and weeks and years.
I will live long and watch over you forever.

I only weep when storms cleanse the land,
and we are torn from earth.
But when the hard wind is past, stillness will return,
and we will continue to bless you with shade from the sun,
and shelter from the rain.

I rejoice in every morning. I rejoice in every night.
I wait for you to come and share your heart.
Your touch against my hard bark
reminds me that I was human once too,

and it is so wonderful, to talk to you,
you of the rare humans, who can hear my voice.
I will tell you my name. I am "Tree," I am all trees.

I will name you now, now that you know my voice.
You are "Walking Leaf."

Like my leaves that I give birth to and let go of,
you also, were born at the tip of your mother's branch.
You have chosen me, and I have chosen you,
and every blade of grass, to be your path.

I will speak in the language,
that knows how to find its way,
into the soul of a human,
and you will listen.

You will speak in the language,
that knows how to find its way,
into the soul of a tree,
and I will listen.

Stand close Walking Leaf.
Hear the sound of the world breathing...

Stand close Walking Leaf.
Know what is in the soul...

I will shine like a beacon from within your heart,
as you walk through the weather of this world.

Eon

When we were little rocks we used to think,
It will be great when we can walk,

and then we were trees and blew in the wind wondering,

"When?"

One morning we woke,
and put our feet over the edge of the bed.

On that same day outside the window,
a Little Bird felt its mother nudge it out of the nest,
and fluttered down through the warm spring to touch the earth.

And right about then, the plumbers truck pulled into the
driveway, and we shook hands and I showed him into the kitchen.

We had to push the black hole out of the way,
to fix the leak in the sink because the universe was dripping down
the drain.

And it would be sad to have all the guests at the table with no
stars to fill their glasses.

For what would they toast, with only air.

But never could a toast could be sweeter,
than with an empty glass.

The purity of its sound, ringing into the other side of the world.

And if our glasses should be empty,
then we should know thirst,
and see into our simple hands.

Sitting there, like the God I never knew,
I would recognize you then,
and reach out my hand.

We would talk until we were full,
and settle in, to do the laundry together.

We would shake the sheets,
until all the little animals rained out
and found their place in the world.

Birds would tumble into the sky,
and fish would wiggle into the sea,
and frogs would flop into the mud and think…

to rest in the mud along the full river is such a comfort,

and the little rocks would think,
It will be great when we can walk.

And the trees were wondering, "When?"

And we put our feet over the edge of the bed,

and the Little Bird was so frightened, but flapped its wings,
and landed on the grass of soft brown earth.

Spirit of Crow

Clouds and stars pass through Spirit of Crow.
Spirit of Crow does not become cold or warm.
Middle of the day on Earth is quiet,
yes, very quiet middle of day.

Seeing crow on Earth, "I am that,
that which flies on Earth and that which is Spirit of Crow."

Spirit of All: "Can Spirit of Crow peel an orange?"
Spirit of Crow: "What is an orange?"
"Do you know what round is?"
"I do not know what round is."
"Do you want to know what round is?"
 "Why would I want to know what round is?"
"Because, then I could tell you what an orange is."

"What is it to peel?" Spirit of Crow asked.
Spirit of all answered, "It is to take what is on the outside off."
"What is off?"
"To release your claws from branch to fly."
"I peel when I fly?"
"No, you have taken your claws off the branch.
 Your claws hold the branch, then they do not hold the branch."
"What is it to hold or to not hold the branch?"
"It is to be held by the earth, or held by the wind."

"I know what it is to fly or not to fly. Is not to fly round?"
 "Do you wish to know what round is?" Spirit of All asked.
 "What is wishing?" Spirit of Crow asked.

"It is to think that breath is not enough."

"Of what do you speak Spirit of All?
My eyes see the day and the night of Earth.
My breath and feathers are of the wind.
Why do you speak of the orange
and of breath that is not enough?"

"Because the orange exists."

"There are many things that exist.
Do not speak of these other things, Spirit of All.
I am of the sun and the wind," Spirit of Crow uttered.
"I have never left what I am, allow me to remain."

Middle of day on earth is quiet,
yes, very quiet middle of day.

Seeing crows on Earth,
Spirit of Crow utters,
"I am that,
that which flies on Earth and that which is Spirit of Crow."

Breaking

The other me waits. He is sitting at the table.
He has carried a weight for a long time.

I come in the door and put down my shoulder bag.
It is a shock to see him there.

"Would you like to talk now," he asks.

I am silent.

I am standing on the sand.
The slow wash of shores lapping wave
brushes past my naked feet and pulls back into the sea.

I know what it means to talk to him.
I will give up everything.

He looks at me kindly.
I sit across from him.

I close my eyes.
He reaches across the table, and takes my hand.

Picture

Cross-legged, the lotus pose. Still.
The window and fireplace, gentle anchors.

Sun's warm glow,
an amber paintbrush.

Your face,
the most beautiful soft canvas for light to find its home.

The couch and carpet, lamps and paintings,
the carefully placed decorative objects,
they all share their presence, soft and muted, glowing.

The room has become still, except for the rise and fall
of your chest, and the sound of your breath.

And what joy it brings me,
to hear the sound of your breath,
knowing you are here in life.

Your being silently floats like little waves of fire.
An almost visible essence shimmering off the surface
of your skin.

This picture, beautiful… moves,

and I feel a kind of tearing,
like something being ripped softly, with no sound.
The essence of our union, moving slowly away.
My heart dissolving.

Dream of Broken Feathers

There is a dream.
It rests on the shore.
It is pulled into the sea, and washed up again.

The seagulls grab it and hope to be born human.
But they fight over it until it is torn,
and they must remain only birds.

At night it is like a light on the beach.
You would be frightened, knowing that nothing glows like
that.
You can see it through the foamy shallow wave washing over.
It's light soft and muted like a beautiful thought about to
become real.

But like the sea gulls coming close to pull it apart,
your curiosity brings you close too,
and seeing you, a big standing creature,
it moves away.

You felt something in your heart, a yearning cry,
"don't go," you quietly hoped.

And it heard,
and lit up the whole ocean because it heard,
there it was, every living thing under the sea,
holding itself open to you.

"Am I seeing this?" you wondered, blinking, and it was still
there, glorious now, revealing even the connection beyond.

You felt yourself let go of something, but before you knew what you were letting go of, you could no longer remember your name and felt the stars inside your chest and looked up to see the stars above you because they were talking to you now,

but there was no above,
just the faintest outline of a shore where you were standing,
and the most beautiful shade of ocean, lit up.

Little scars of dirt washed from your skin,
and little scars of dirt washed from your memory.
It felt so good to let them go.

You were crying and became pure,
and the essence of your being opened.
For one moment, you knew that you were everything.

***

When I saw you,
wafting like spring through the door,
and blowing out the window into the sun,

I had hoped to touch you,
and we all reached out...

At night, you are glowing through a veil,
dancing like promise on the other side.

We are floating out of our lives,
sailing almost close enough to touch,
but you see us and dissolve into a sun
that leaves us drifting in bliss.

We have never had this dream before.
And now, sitting on the edge of our bed,
we remember, and open into tears, alone.

***

There is a feather on the grass.
The morning light speaks like the mother and father I never had.

"Oh dear friend, dear friend, you are welcome in my embrace.
My light, upon this grass, upon you.

Please do not leave dear friend, stay in my morning light,
I have so much I want to tell you.
Did I show you my sparrow?

Your skin… that is what I am brushing near,
that is how I know it is you.

It is falling from the sky,
yes there it is, the feather from my tail.

You can keep it, my whole life is there."

Sailing Home

I quietly end here.

Thank you, for these many breaths,
and for my feet upon the earth.

Thank you, for the branches gathered together,
and the hands that made them into shelter.

Thank you for our reflection in the water,
as we danced across our lives.

Thank you

Thank you to my family and friends who have patiently listened for so long: Herb Forsberg, Frank Cantor, Jim Mullen, Tony Forma, Mike Barry, and Ed Ballen.

Thank you to Vinny Dacquino, who began the writers group in Mahopac NY, a space where all dreams are welcome, and to all the members there.

Thank you to the weekend writers group whose members have been more helpful and supportive than I ever could have imagined: Dana Chipkin, Heather Fullerton, Heidi Stein, Barry Antokolitz, Jennifer Ciotta, Andy Campbell, and Bob Zaslow.

And thank you to Lorra Hoffman, who listened to all of mywork, and was always kind and encouraging.

I remember a moment when I was nine.
I was standing on the front lawn.
A question entered my mind.
"What am I doing here?"

Now, many years later,
I am more at peace with the question.

I live in New York State,
where the seasons remind me,
that everything returns home.

- Jeff Edrich

www.ingramcontent.com/pod-product-compliance
Lightning Source LLC
Chambersburg PA
CBHW051825040426
42447CB00006B/368